3 NEW YORK POETS

Charles North

Tony Towle

Paul Violi

3 NEW YORK POETS

Charles North
Tony Towle
Paul Violi

EDITED WITH ESSAYS ON THE WRITERS BY

Andrew McCarron

FOREWORD BY

John Koethe

Station Hill
of Barrytown

Published by Station Hill Press, Inc., 120 Station Hill Road, Barrytown, NY 12507, as a project of the Institute for Publishing Arts, Inc., in Barrytown, New York, a not-for-profit, tax-exempt organization [501(c)(3)], supported in part by grants from the New York State Council on the Arts, a state agency.

Online catalogue: www.stationhill.org
e-mail: publishers@stationhill.org
Interior and cover design by Susan Quasha.

Cover image: "6th Avenue Night with Traffic" (2008), Yvonne Jacquette. Pastel on paper, 28 x 22 inches. Courtesy of the artist and DC Moore Gallery, New York.

Photo Credits: David Kelley

The works of Charles North, Tony Towle and Paul Violi are used by permission as follows: *What It Is Like* © 2011 by Charles North, by permission of Hanging Loose Press. *The History of the Invitation: New and Selected Poems 1963–2000* © 2001 by Tony Towle, by permission of Hanging Loose Press. *The Curious Builder* © 1993 by Paul Violi, by permission of Hanging Loose Press. *Overnight* © 2007 by Paul Violi, by permission of Hanging Loose Press. *The Tame Magpie* © 2014 by Paul Violi, by permission of Hanging Loose Press. All attempts have been made to acquire permissions for early works not published by Hanging Loose Press.

The author would like to kindly acknowledge the editorial support of the following individuals: Suzanne Ouellette, Michelle Fine, John Koethe, Charles North, Tony Towle, Paul Violi, Sam Truitt, Charles Stein, Bill Zavatsky, and Elisa Dragu.

Library of Congress Cataloging-in-Publication Data
McCarron, Andrew.
  Three New York Poets : Charles North, Tony Towle, Paul Violi / by Andrew McCarron ; foreword by John Koethe.
    pages cm
  ISBN 978-1-58177-146-6
  1. American poetry—New York (State)—New York—History and criticism.
  2. American poetry—20th century—History and criticism. 3. North, Charles, 1941—-Criticism and interpretation. 4. Towle, Tony, 1939—-Criticism and interpretation. 5. Koethe, John, 1945—-Criticism and interpretation. 6. Poets, American—Homes and haunts—New York (State)—New York. 7. New York (N.Y.)—Intellectual life—20th century. I. Title.
  PS255.N5M35 2015
  811'.540997471—dc23
                          2014037933

Manufactured in the United States of America

CONTENTS

Paul Violi

FOREWORD

ANDREW MCCARRON'S *Three New York Poets*, a psychological, biographical and literary study of the poets Charles North, Tony Towle and Paul Violi, is a substantially revised version of the dissertation for which he received a doctorate in psychology from The Graduate Center of The City University of New York in 2010. After a fascinating and largely autobiographical introduction, McCarron devotes a section to each of the three poets, consisting of a generous selection of his work, a biographical and psychological sketch based on extensive interviews, and a brief critical account of the poetry.

It's a unique book, whose importance strikes me as threefold. First, it draws attention to the works of three excellent poets associated with the so-called New York School of Poetry, each of whom has received a decent amount of recognition but deserves to be more widely known. Second, it enhances our understanding of what seems to me the most important grouping in any taxonomy of contemporary American poetry, the New York School itself, which despite its renown (or notoriety), remains difficult to characterize and delineate. And third, it offers a vivid sense of the relationships between each poet's identity and development as a poet and his everyday domestic and psychological life, something usually reserved for writers who achieve sufficient stature to warrant full-scale biographies after their deaths.

North, Towle and Violi are commonly thought of as poets of the New York School, but the fact that their works (which I'll turn to shortly) have so little in common ought to be an indication of how problematic that classification is. According to legend (which happens to be true), the term "poets of the New York School" was coined by John Bernard Myers to refer to John Ashbery, Kenneth Koch,

Frank O'Hara and James Schuyler (the subjects of David Lehman's book *The Last Avant-Garde*). All three had been friends at Harvard in the 1940s and hung around and drank with many of the New York painters who constituted the "school" Myers refers to, with no suggestion that the works of the poets had much in common beyond being published by Myers himself through the Tibor de Nagy Gallery. (For an excellent historical account of the aesthetic milieu in which they moved, see Douglas Crase's introduction to *Painters & Poets: Tibor de Nagy Gallery*). The idea that American poetry should be divided into distinctive schools was given impetus by the publication in 1960 of Donald Allen's *The New American Poetry 1945–1960* (along with its academic foil, Donald Hall, Robert Pack and Louis Simpson's *New Poets of England and America*, published in 1957), which broke the poets it included into a number of somewhat specious groups or movements, one of which consisted of the four New York figures, along with Barbara Guest and Edward Field.

It is instructive to compare the New York grouping with some of the others to be found on the landscape of mid-twentieth century American poetry: the Black Mountain poets, the San Francisco Renaissance, the Beats, as well as the group (not usually thought of as a school, and certainly not on Allen's map) consisting of Robert Lowell, John Berryman, Elizabeth Bishop and Randall Jarrell. Some of these were associated with a normative poetics (Charles Olson's "Projective Verse" for the Black Mountain poets) or a strong interest in poetics (the San Francisco Renaissance) or an ethos (the Beats), but in the case of the New York poets these are largely absent (despite a greater interest in modern music and painting than was typical of most American poets, and notwithstanding Frank O'Hara's mock manifesto "Personism" and Kenneth Koch's hilarious rant "Fresh Air"). To my mind the grouping they most resemble is the

Lowell-Berryman-Bishop-Jarrell one, in which the poets were united not by a theoretical outlook but by friendship, shared tastes, geography (at least to some extent) and an appreciation of and an interest in promoting one another's work.

It's only a slight exaggeration to think of the New York School—the "first generation" New York School—as an invention of what's come to be called the second generation New York School, which emerged in the early sixties and consisted of a large number of younger poets, including the Tulsa émigrés Ted Berrigan, Ron Padgett, Joe Brainard and Dick Gallup, as well as poets already in New York like Bill Berkson, Frank Lima, David Shapiro and two of McCarron's subjects, Tony Towle and Charles North. These younger poets revered the works of the older ones and in effect turned what had been an association of poets loosely bound together by friendship and taste into a reified canonical grouping. Towle (both in McCarron's account and in his own marvelous *Memoir*) makes clear what the formation of this second generation involved, which included the approval and friendship of one or more of the original poets (usually, as in his own case, O'Hara or Koch, as Ashbery was still living in Paris and Schuyler was more reclusive than the others). But there were other factors that lent cohesion to this younger group: one being geographical and the other institutional. The ready availability of cheap apartments on the Lower East Side meant that its members could live in close proximity to one another (though McCarron makes clear that not all of them in fact lived downtown), and the establishment of the St. Marks Poetry Project in the mid-sixties, with its regular schedule of readings and workshops, which provided an institutional means for the New York School to perpetuate itself. For example, just as Towle's poetic identity was to a great extent formed by O'Hara's and Koch's classes at The New School, so North's and Violi's identities were formed in

part by a workshop Towle gave at the Poetry Project, and the friend-
ship that developed between the three of them.

It seems to me that it is these personal and historical connections,
rather than anything that might be called a shared poetics, that con-
stitute the New York School as it has persisted now for over half a
century. North's interest in contemporary philosophy informs much
of his work, and some of the ideas associated with the philosopher
Saul Kripke, who is obliquely alluded to in North's diaristic "Sum-
mer of Living Dangerously," help draw the contrast I have in mind.
Kripke is important for (among other things) shifting philosophy
away from the idea that what one is talking about when using a
term (like "the New York School") is determined by a description
or concept associated with it (or here, perhaps, a poetics). Instead,
he argued, it's determined by a network or chain of personal and
historical relationships surrounding the introduction and subsequent
applications of the term. And it seems to me that something like this
view of the New York School is supported by McCarron's study.

The case for a nonthematic view of the New York School is
strengthened by the differences between the works of his three
poets, which are well treated by the essays McCarron appends to
the sections on each poet. North's work is, somewhat paradoxically,
the most conceptual and theoretical but also the most private and
personal of the three. I've mentioned the interest in philosophy that
underlies much of his poetry (Kripke's notion of a rigid designator
makes an appearance towards the end of "Summer of Living Dan-
gerously"), and he's well known for his "Lineups," in which cities,
spices, philosophers, movies, body parts and much else occupy the
places of the players in a baseball lineup. But while North's poems are
conceptually driven, they rarely take the form of sustained, explicit
meditations, and what makes them so personal is the fact that their

conceptual underpinnings remain private, so that the poems have the feel of outward manifestations of sustained trains of thought whose precise contents remain hidden, disguised by an attractive reticence emphasized by McCarron in his psychological study. They are also meticulously crafted, a reflection perhaps of North's musical background, and in their seductive combination of the personal and the private they often put me in mind of John Ashbery's lines from "Some Trees": "Our days put on such reticence/These accents seem their own defense."

Towle's poems, on the other hand, are muscular and autobiographical, with an immediacy and vigor one associates with Frank O'Hara. Yet despite their extensive use of autobiographical material, their relation to his life often remains elusive, since their development is governed by surrealist and associative impulses as well, as the in long poem "Autobiography." A characterization of the difference between Towle's and O'Hara's use of the autobiographical is provided by his friend North, contrasting O'Hara's "I do this I do that" poems with "Towle's procedure, [which] is something like 'I do this I think that, now I am that, now that has become this, now I'm considering what I just thought and felt about that, etc.'"

Finally, Violi's work can be both poignant and hilarious, a respect in which he resembles his friend and fellow Columbia teacher Kenneth Koch. It sometimes takes the form of a bravura public performance, as in his much-anthologized "Index," in which the life of a hapless fictional painter is depicted by the entries in the index of his biography, or in "Counterman," in which a customer's order of a roast beef sandwich is formulated in classical architectural terms, resulting in a dazzling verbal construction of absurd beauty.

Three New York Poets provides excellent, if necessarily truncated, accounts of the works of its subjects, but what is unique about the book is its portraits of the poets themselves, portraits that are partly biographical and partly psychological. I suppose in some sense our understanding of a poet's work should be self-contained, but because we value poetry we value poets too, and seek an understanding of them as well as of their work. And while at some level—at some level—the life of a serious poet is centered on poetry, the fact is that one writes it in the midst of life, a life that includes so much more than poetry, which we're in danger of losing sight of if our interests are exclusively aesthetic.

What I find most fascinating about McCarron's study is the way he situates the development of each poet's work and poetic identity in the context of the course of his personal and domestic life. It's moving to see North's conceptually intense work in the context of a family life centered on his wife and children; or to place Towle's vigorous and confident poems in the context of a life filled with personal and physical hardship; or to realize that beyond Violi's New York-centered poetic identity he inhabited an entire domestic world outside the city. "Purists will object" (in the words of a John Ashbery title) that this is of little relevance to poetry itself. But then purists are likely to have little interest in "what it is like" (the title of North's new and selected poems) to be a poet, which is precisely McCarron's concern, and one that the reader quickly comes to share.

I said at the outset that North, Towle and Violi have achieved a decent amount of recognition but that they deserve to be better known. I stand by that, but it raises questions about the nature of poetic reputations. Someone once quipped that being a famous poet doesn't entail being famous, and it's not at all clear what the significance of being a well-known poet really is. I've suggested that the New York School is more like an environment than an ideology, and while some of the figures inhabiting that environment are widely recognized outside it—the four original figures, of course, and a few of the later figures (Ron Padgett and Anne Waldman, for instance, are Chancellors of the Academy of American Poets)—the fact remains that most poets associated with the New York School, including many of the best ones, aren't widely known beyond it. What the New York School represents is a world within which the work of poets like North, Towle and Violi is revered, respected and appreciated on its own terms, and it's certainly not obvious that this is a less significant form of recognition than the one associated with the world of reading circuits and M.F.A. programs. It's hard to know what the "world" of contemporary American poetry really amounts to, for it's so dispersed, so abstract, so virtual—by contrast with the image that lingers for me from *Three New York Poets*, of some poets at a bar hanging out together talking.

—John Koethe

INTRODUCTION

I WROTE my first poem in the eighth grade, a tortured lament about a girl named Caroline who hurt my feelings. The allure of poetry reemerged when as a high school junior I read *On The Road* and *Howl*. I liked the intensity of the Beats, especially the musicality of their lines, and how they mention one another by name in their works. Wanting to be like them, I remember stapling together a chapbook of original poems called *Nine Valley Songs* during my freshman year at Bard College. The summer between freshman and sophomore year was significant because I discovered the writing of John Ashbery. I picked up a copy of his book, *And the Stars Were Shining*, after applying and being selected for his workshop the following fall. My favorite lines appear in one of the final stanzas of the long title poem that ends the collection:

> So—if you want to come with me,
> or just pull at my sleeve, let them make that discovery.
> Summer won't end in your lap,
> nor are the stars more casual than usual.

The language was abstract, but familiar emotionally, like hearing an ancient melody in a new song. The meaning of the words was mysterious and funny at the same time, and contained objects from the world that can be seen and from the world that can't. Getting to know the master himself was like reading one of his more enigmatic poems. He was then seventy years old, warm, unpretentious, and appealingly bizarre. I recall the piercing intensity of his blue eyes, and how they focused on their subject with bright curiosity. Sometimes his eyes would tear up when he heard a poem that moved him.

Other times he seemed uninterested in anything other than the music of his private thoughts. He said that a poem didn't have to make sense, it could be about anything, and it could be made up of sound bites and language fragments from the outside world. He told us in his distinctive upstate New York twang about hearing an elderly woman say to her miniature dog, "Come on, *dear*. Come on, *dear*," and rushing home to write a poem about it.

That fall I walked to a landscape park near Bard called Poet's Walk. While coming up from the river through the woods, I dreamed up a series of lines and rushed home to write a two-page poem (my longest at that point) called "The Long View." It was fresh, immediate, and full of everything of that moment. Something sounded through my consciousness like the screech of a red tail hawk. It's hard to explain, but I didn't want the feeling to stop, and so my practice of writing increased. All well and good, but lacking a poetic community other than a handful of classmates, I didn't have the foggiest idea of how one went about becoming a poet. There was no such thing as a poet where I came from.

Following some advice given by Ashbery to the entire workshop, I sent a few poems, including "The Long View," to a list of well-known poetry journals. Several months later I received my first rejection letters. Clearly, it wasn't going to be so easy. I waited and waited, but the genius committee didn't show up on my doorstep with a book contract. And for whatever reason, writing poems by myself wasn't enough. A dream of being "discovered" charged me with starry-eyed hope for literary recognition.

Somewhere around then I checked out a copy of David Lehman's *The Last Avant-Garde: The Making of the New York School of Poets.* I found out things about Ashbery that he didn't reveal in class. For example, he was famous, seen by critics like Harold Bloom as the most important American poet since Wallace Stevens. W.H. Auden chose his first book, *Some Trees*, for the Yale Series of Younger Poets in 1956. I also learned that he had been part of a group of poets who met as undergraduates at Harvard in the late forties. The others were Frank O'Hara and Kenneth Koch. A fourth, James Schuyler, met them later on in New York City. These men were at the center of a group that went on to shape the landscape of post-WWII American poetry. Lehman defined them in terms of their relationships with one another, the influence of French surrealist poetry and abstract expressionism upon their works, and New York City itself. The backdrop for their meetings was a rundown bar at University Place and Eighth Street called the Cedar Tavern. A preferred watering hole for Abstract Expressionist painters like Pollack and de Kooning in the fifties and early sixties, the Cedar became a regular hangout for Ashbery and his friends, in addition to a Village bar called the San Remo. The poets and painters drank copious amounts of alcohol, talked up a storm, and exchanged work. Lehman's book wrapped up the experience into an exciting mythology that I dreamed of having in my own time. I imagined that membership in the artistic community that Lehman described would validate my existence, granting me a sense of identity and purpose that could elevate me above the suburban subdivisions and social conformities of my middle-class upbringing.

Eager for guidance, I invited myself over to Ashbery's Victorian home in Hudson in the fall of 1998. The house was huge, and my memory of it consists of wood paneling, parlors, and stained glass. I asked him questions about the New York School and left with an armful of books by poets active around New York City, where Ashbery and his partner, David Kermani, lived during the week. One of the books was by Charles North, and there were others by Ann Lauterbach and Ron Padgett. Many of the poets were involved with something called the Saint Mark's Poetry Project, which Ashbery mentioned to me, suggesting I check it out myself if I ever were to move to New York.

I moved to Manhattan four years later to take a job teaching Religion and English at a private school on the Upper West Side. In a simple twist of fate, two of my colleagues happened to be involved in the downtown poetry scene. One was an English teacher named Bill Zavatsky who had been one of Kenneth Koch's students at Columbia in the late sixties. He once ran a small press in New York City called SUN that published a number of New York School writers. Bill, who had been on the periphery of the Saint Mark's scene for many years, told me about its history. Founded by Paul Blackburn in 1966, the Project had been facilitating workshops, hosting readings, publishing poets' work, and maintaining archives for over four decades. Bill explained that many former students and younger friends of Ashbery, O'Hara, Koch, and Schuyler congregated there for readings and book launches. Until his death in the early eighties, the larger-than-life poet Ted Berrigan was a commanding presence on the scene. Among many others who were active in the Project's early days were Jim Carroll, Anselm Hollo, Ron Padgett, Anne Waldman, Bernadette Mayer, and Lewis Warsh.

The other friend I made through my work was a recent Columbia graduate and former student of Kenneth Koch named Justin Jamail. He was biding his time before going off to graduate school by working in the school's development office. During his senior year at Columbia, he'd taken a workshop with a poet named Paul Violi. Justin shared some of Paul's work with me, in addition to the work of Paul's close friends, Charles North (with whom I was already familiar), and Tony Towle. All three had connections to the first generation of the New York School. Paul had taken over Kenneth Koch's

"Imaginative Writing" class after his death from leukemia in 2001. Tony had been a good friend of Frank O'Hara before the poet's tragic death in 1966. And North was a favorite of Ashbery and had also been relatively close to the eccentric James Schuyler through the seventies and eighties. Justin was in the habit of meeting Paul and Tony every Tuesday night at the Fish Bar in the East Village. Paul was teaching a workshop at the New School and liked to unwind before making the hour-plus drive back to the house he shared with his wife in Putnam County. I was invited to join them and began doing so regularly.

Paul (1944–2011) had a vigorous presence. He was a virile sixty with dark hair and seemed to live on cigarettes and coffee. I was put at immediate ease by his warmth, humor, and intelligence. After drinking a few beers and chuckling his way through several absurdist stories, he'd smoke a cigarette and then head off with a steaming cup of bodega coffee in hand. Despite the long day he'd put in scuttling between Columbia, The New School, and NYU, he didn't seem the least bit tired, trotting around the corner and disappearing into the night to find his car. Paul was the adventurer of the three: committed to a frenetic lifestyle of fun and duty, combining family with friends, and poetry with employment. He had a twinkle in his eye and a cosmically reassuring smile.

Tony (born 1939) was a tall, distinguished-looking man with a cane and a trim gray beard. A few years older than Paul, he walked cautiously and had a slight tremor in his hands. His voice was simultaneously reflective, urbane, and sardonic. A professional editor, he was the historian of the three, brimming with detailed personal anecdotes about Frank O'Hara and Kenneth Koch, complete with place names and dates. Hanging out with Tony was like sitting in a minor-league dugout with an old-timer who'd been sent down. He was happy to be in the game but yearned for a time that had long since passed, back when he was writing more consistently and earning more praise for his efforts. He felt slighted by people who passed him over for publications and readings.

Charles (born 1941) only came to the Fish Bar for drinks once. He'd recently undergone a successful open-heart surgery to repair a leaky aortic valve and was generally measured when it came to socializing. He was athletic, lean, of medium height, and had dark-rimmed glasses and graying hair. Whereas Tony was an entertaining monologist, Charles was an outstanding listener, smiling and shaking his head attentively when others spoke. He had a philosophical way of framing ideas and questions and took care in his choice of words. A skilled teacher, he worked as the Poet-in-Residence at Pace University. None of the three had the bad boy swagger that I associated with a bunch of "city poets" hanging out in a bar. They were thoughtful, good-humored, and conservatively dressed in collared shirts and sport coats.

I kept in touch with Paul, Tony, and Charles over the years that followed, occasionally meeting up for drinks or dinner. Whenever any of them gave a reading, I did my best to be there. After most of these readings, there'd be a gathering at a nearby restaurant. The assembled group usually included my colleague Justin, his partner, Amber Reed, and their friend from Columbia, Davey Volner. Tony's girlfriend, Diane, and Charles' wife, Paula, would often join the group too, as would Paul's close friends David and Alex Kelley. Michael Davis, a friend of Tony's who lived in Princeton, would frequently take the train in for the evening. Paul's wife, Ann, would very occasionally make the journey down from Putnam County. Appetizers and entrees would be ordered, and glasses of wine would be raised in honor of the evening's reader.

Tony, Charles, and Paul had been socializing and sharing work for nearly four decades when I met them. In many respects their linked story had begun in and around the mythology of the Cedar Tavern. Tony had moved to New York from Washington, D.C., in 1960. An aspiring young poet, he began hanging out at the Cedar and met Frank O'Hara and eventually Kenneth Koch. O'Hara took a liking to him and ushered the younger man into an exciting world of art openings, book signings, and parties. What felt like the beginning, though, was actually the end. The Cedar closed its doors in 1963, and three years later O'Hara was tragically struck by a dune buggy on Fire Island in the early morning hours of July 24th and died of a ruptured liver the following day. The loss of Frank O'Hara would continue to haunt Tony's poetry and life.

The founding of the Poetry Project at Saint Mark's Church in 1966 signaled a new chapter for the downtown poetry scene. And in the late sixties Anne Waldman and her first husband, Lewis Warsh, kept an open house at their Saint Mark's Place apartment for the poets and artists of their generation, the vast majority of whom were involved on some level with the Poetry Project. Tony had social capital within this crowd since he, like Bill Berkson, had a personal relationship with Frank O'Hara and a number of Frank's poet and painter friends. Also, his second book was published by the Tibor de Nagy Gallery, which also published early works by the first generation of the New York School. These things set him apart from many of his contemporaries, as did winning the second annual Frank O'Hara prize from Columbia University Press in 1970.

In 1969 Tony was asked to teach two consecutive semesters of workshops at Saint Mark's, one in the fall and one in the spring. He ran them loosely and told participants that they were welcome to give him up to six pages of poems per week for him to comment on, a protocol practiced in workshops he'd taken with Koch and O'Hara some years earlier. It was through these workshops that Tony met Paul Violi and Charles North. Paul joined the workshop during the fall, and Charles, who had been abroad for several months, joined that spring. Tony immediately noticed that they had talent and "were as good as I was, or at least well on their way." In the tradition of O'Hara, Tony invited his students to come with him to a local hangout for pizza and drinks. It was during these high-energy rap sessions that the three poets became close friends and artistic collaborators.

Charles describes having a creative breakthrough as a result of Tony's workshop. He was at a point where he had considered giving up poetry, so Tony's entrance into his life was important. He quickly fell into the habit of showing Tony just about everything he wrote and receiving helpful feedback. Similarly, Paul recalled being inspired by Tony's mentorship and greatly enjoyed the companionship: "It seemed like the three of us were just naturally compatible friends, in terms of humor and our take on poetry. We became friends very quickly. There were a lot of after-reading and after-workshop get-togethers at bars. We were interested in literature, you know, not just the poetry scene. And our humor—our senses of humor—complemented one another. We had a lot of fun, and I also learned a great deal from them."

Over the decades that followed, the three men raised families, endured misfortune and loss, and scrambled around for steady work. Through it all they composed as much new poetry as time and inspiration would allow and almost always let each other read what they'd created. In the late eighties the New York-based Hanging Loose Press, run by the poet Bob Hershon and three colleagues, began publishing the poets' work: Paul's in 1988, Charles' in 1989, and Tony's in 2001. Hanging Loose continues to this day to publish their books.

The big poetry prizes and major book deals eluded them, however. There were feelings of letdown over the years, quiet resentments that far less deserving poets were being heralded as major voices in American arts and letters. Outside a relatively small circle of fellow poets, M.F.A. students, and poetry enthusiasts, their publications were met with the silence of a literate public that read less and less verse. And those who did read tended to shy away from "difficult" poetry. Still, Charles, Tony, and Paul published books, gave readings, taught, and won a number of more modest prizes and honors.

In 2008 I was a few years into a doctoral program in psychology at the Graduate Center of CUNY and trying to decide upon a dissertation topic. Having been trained in personality psychology and psychobiography, I came up with the idea of conducting lengthy interviews with Tony, Charles, and Paul. I wanted to find out when each had begun referring to himself as a poet and how that identification played a role in shaping their lives. Jean-Paul Sartre wrote about how people's lives are oriented around progressive projects. "For us," Sartre writes, "man is characterized above all by his going beyond a situation, and by what he succeeds in making of what he has been made." I was interested in how poetry helped Tony, Charles, and Paul to make something that reflected their innermost hopes and desires. I wanted to find out why each of them was called to poetry.

All three were heterosexual white men born into upwardly mobile middle class households in or around New York City. All three tried out a few other vocations before settling on writing. Central to their artistic awakenings was a specific place (New York City), a poetic lineage (the New York School of Poetry), a specific literary/art scene (the Poetry Project), and one another. Being a poet required more than simply writing; it required recognition from a community that was notoriously competitive and hard to break into.

In his 1991 *Atlantic* essay, *Can Poetry Matter?*, Dana Gioia reflected on how poetry had become a highly specialized occupation of a small and relatively isolated group of writers, editors, and academics who often privileged political connections over the merit of the work itself. Even though there were more M.F.A. writing programs and poetry journals than ever before in literary history, the general readership of poetry was at an all-time low. For the modern American poet, becoming well-connected was a necessary part of getting into print, receiving awards, and finding poetry-related employment. A bohemian life dedicated to writing without an active investment in the poetry marketplace promised little in the way of exposure, let alone a sustainable existence.

Tony, Charles, and Paul shared a common thread when it came to the role that older mentors played in the development of their poetic reputations. A young poet wasn't a "poet" until he earned the respect of an older writer in the community. Tony, for example, speaks of *becoming* a poet in the years after he became friends with Frank O'Hara:

> By the end of the year [1963], I felt that my poems were finally getting somewhere. I felt no such confidence about the rest of my life. I was barely making enough money to live on. Romance was nonexistent. Whether my poetry was an escape or refuge from what I should have been squarely facing was beside the point: I was impelled to continue. Even though it would be another five years—only after I had a book published—before I would answer the question 'What do you do?' with 'I'm a poet'—it was *then*, as 1963 drew to a close, that I knew it was so.

Had he not met Frank O'Hara, he may never have thought of himself in these terms. And Tony played a similar role in launching the poetic careers of Charles and Paul through their participation in his writing workshop. Both would go on to teach their own workshops over the decades that followed, and Paul would even direct the Poetry Project for a time in the eighties.

I learned these things over the course of several years of conversations and interviews. I spoke with Tony the most. Our wide-ranging conversations, each between three and five hours long, occurred over dinner and drinks at a restaurant around the corner from the Tribeca apartment he shares with his girlfriend. I interviewed Charles in his living room, usually in the late afternoon. With Paul I conducted five sprawling interviews at my apartment on the Upper West Side of Manhattan during the early evening hours before Paul's hour-long drive home to Putnam Valley after teaching classes at The New School and/or NYU.

I also drew upon other sources for my research. Although no major biographical work to date has been done on the three, reviews, interviews, and critical treatments of the New York School are available. Additionally, Tony published a one-hundred-page memoir of his life from 1960–1963, the years immediately before and after he moved to New York City and began writing poetry. I knew Tony, Charles, and Paul for about five years before embarking on this project, and so I'd learned a good deal about them by just being around. I also acquainted myself with each poet's corpus of work, which, in addition to collections of poetry, included prose publications, chapbooks, poetry pamphlets, art books, collaborations, broadsides, essays, published letters, and, in the case of Tony and Charles, a volume of selected poems.

The life studies that follow aren't objective biographies, nor are they comprehensive. They are attempts on my part to represent how these three men went about answering the question, *When did you start thinking of yourself as a poet?* I begin each poet's chapter with a selection of poems followed by a two-part essay that recounts his life story, pieced together from lengthy interview transcripts, followed by some critical reflections on his poems.

The reason I was drawn to the life stories of three older poets peeking out from behind the long shadows of a previous generation of giants was the same reason I came to New York City. High up in the rafters of my consciousness hovered a memory of something I had seen, or heard, or felt as a kid. It was shiny and as light as helium, a feeling that turned into a quest that had little to do with what passed as "the real world." That feeling survived the straitening conformities of maturation by hiding out in words. And in large and small ways, these words transformed the world into a magical realm of discovery and possibility.

I can't say that I found what I was looking for by shining a light into the lives of Charles, Tony, and Paul, because, in the end, I was looking for something metaphysical—an explanation for the magic behind the irresistible compulsion to write. All three men clearly had deeply personal reasons for writing, but the experience for each was inexorably linked with "making it" in commercial terms. This unpleasant reality frustrated them, but they also unwittingly appraised themselves based upon the accolades they had or hadn't received over the years. This isn't to say, however, that deeper aspects of who they are, and why they've written what they've written, weren't revealed, or at least hinted at. But such revelations came only in hints and guesses about some incommunicable or far too private truth.

One year after I defended my dissertation, Paul was taken ill quite suddenly and died of aggressive pancreatic cancer. With Paul gone, Tony and Charles stopped meeting as regularly as they once did. The absence of his humor and charisma changed their social dynamic, and a decision was made to stop their monthly meetings at the Café Loup in Greenwich Village. It just wouldn't be the same without him.

Coincidentally, sometime during the year leading up to Paul's death, and without even realizing it, I stopped self-identifying as a poet. The constant rejection, the jockeying, and the fragile need to be admired muted the internal stirrings that had once compelled me down that path. Although I continue to write privately, the baggage that came with the identity made me feel anything but poetic. I had finally gotten my first collection of poems into print, in addition to publishing individual poems in good journals. Much to my surprise, though, I found myself drifting away from a feeling I assumed would be inside me forever.

Charles North

POEM

When you consider how Europe flashes by
like a vowel, and in obsolete whispers
or in uttering in a whisper, talking or saying
privately or secretly and having a curved
outside or form especially like the Joan of Arc
of a flame, or characterized by full spontaneous
movement not in a circle, not cramped or limited
but free & vigorous in motion as an integer—
then anything within the sphere of a number
globe or ring, a group such as positions
or any course ending where it began, is as
complete as you are, and ends where you began,
loosely or simultaneously reprieved (like air)
or the space below, which is perfect, less rare

CHARLES NORTH

TO THE BOOK

Open poetry died with Whitman.
Closed poetry died with Yeats.
Natural poetry was born and died with Lorca
And Clare, also with France's Jean de Meung.
The feeling of being caught (and held)
Is reproduced in the sonneteers of the English Renaissance,
With the exception of one very great poet whose work opens.
Cars, lights, and love belong to Catullus
And to the Chinese, and to the death of symbolism
In Henry Vaughan, naturalism's decay
In Stephen Crane, the growth and moribundity
Of obsessive sex à la the works of Ponge and MacPherson
And in Basho, Li Po, and Fitzgerald (and Khayam).
Mannerism in Emerson, consumption in Leopardi,
Sleep and poetry in Sappho, Nash, Swift,
Gibran and Coleridge; decadence,
Humor, Platonism, hysteria, line endings, skald,
And the quality of unearthly, though unhysterical, beauty
In John Skelton and Anne Bradstreet; François
De Malherbe and Vosnesensky, what qualities are dead
In you that will have their rebirth here?

LINES

As farming and evening,
taken together, are
the same thing. The morning air

dents a jar of tulips
and interurban affairs are wasted
with the dispatch of an elegant theory.

The empowerment
of leaders begins its arduous journey
through permanent display, pink

a parade of points, green
turning out products, linking
highway to art to meta-abrasive.

But the free movement through
elevated channels causes the scale to fold,
the council to abandon.

SONG

I am pressed up against you
Like air pressed up against the sky
The carpenter ants are at work on the bearing beams
O bearing beams

Like air pressed up against the sky
So will the hills attain
O bearing beams
Disguised as cows touched here and there with stray sunlight

So will the hills attain
Their dole of cloud-famished city
Disguised as cows touched here and there with stray sunlight
In short we frequently get tangled

Their dole of cloud-famished city
Each bordering river inflects with something of its own
In short we frequently get tangled
Which has nothing on confusion itself

Each bordering river inflects with something of its own
Sticking piecemeal above the regret
Which has nothing on confusion itself
Save that it lowers the boom on customary behavior

Sticking piecemeal above the regret
The word I have for you flowers in several places
Save that it lowers the boom on customary behavior
Like October's fiery rip

THE DAWN

The dawn was contagious, spreading
rapidly about the heavens. —Flann O'Brien

TO BE

Immortal.

ONLY

A pencil line of sunlight is climbing
Straight up the chimney, stopping about two inches
From the top

IMPINGING

On a template of powder blue without end

IT FOLLOWS THAT

Compressed, highlighted and seductively polished
Within a naturally limited theater of operations
Snow or sleet, the occasional burst rising to produce
A new century

SPACE IS FURIOUS

Still beneath the roof of your hair
The dials keynote our penchant for constructing

Problems that test the ground underneath, reflecting wintergreen
All the way up to buildings including several different
   varieties

     THE WAY IT PRODDED

All nabis and all
Oily charm, conveniently summarized
Which is not to say without vague hopes of escape into
   the evening sky

     PARTICULARLY THE DAWN

Approximately fifteen feet back from where
The houses, secure at least temporarily from flattening,
Peered out over what had been left of the horizon—
   that is,
What hadn't been previously usurped
By the "developers"

     WHEN LAST WE

Met.

     EVEN NOW

Your arms are the unencumbered coastline

LIKE AN ALTO SAXOPHONE

With cherries in the bell. It isn't
Selected cities

LIMNING

And individuating green light; as though some passing
  cloud

SOFTER THAN LASERS TO STYROFOAM

Not exactly carried aloft like the anthem of autumn
But a rubric of sopping wet air that
Has aimed its complement in a forthcoming way

A SWEET SMELL

Like the armpit
Of an angel

OR PERFECTION OF THE LIFE

The earth is
Pulled up to the surface, or
The surface is pulled down till it hits; either way
The blue is spooned over lush

WHY I AM NOT A GERMAN ROMANTIC

THE PLACE OF RUNNING BOARDS

If, and it's a big one,
This clumsy desire to be confined to you and you only
Means hammering out the decision
Where all is difficult to see

AS THOUGH EACH FRAGRANT CAUSEWAY

Doubled the space between monsters—I mean trampling
The news from the perspective of summer
Until the only boarder of note sheds quality
In the form of clothespins pushed up towards the thinnest
    leaf

NOT BEING OR BEING NOT BEING

The primroses

OF MY DISCONTENT

Not the shoal
Where we argue the limitless side, but somehow
Swarming down the coal chute to be played
According to those golden notions of equal
And opposite reaction, swallowed up by, at least
In part, the same religious architecture
That works on the mind like feelers, extending even
    into the current

LIKE CARROTS TO HILLS

The gray carrots, and the almost
Maple rolling hills

CHARLES NORTH

THE PHILOSOPHY OF NEW JERSEY

for Jill

Actually the sky appears older than it is. It's 63 or 64 at most, not 75. The part with the cliff face and the yellow crane could be in its early 30s. It wasn't Wallace Stevens who said, "They have cut off my head, and picked out all the letters of the alphabet—all the vowels and consonants—and brought them out through my ears; and then they want me to write poetry! I can't do it!" It was John Clare. Wallace Stevens said—something like—the best poems are the ones you meant to write. That has a nice sound to it, but it's hard to see how he or anyone would know that. It would be hard, for example, to accept the notion that there are ideas one meant to have. Poems underneath every peeling sycamore and inside every file cabinet, along with ideas about poetry and uncountable other ideas.

DAY AFTER DAY THE STORM MOUNTED. THEN IT DISMOUNTED

Suppose I am not the uplifter of all I uplift,
in the same sense that the coal-black sky, scumbled and showing a
   few red streaks,
doesn't exactly equal space.

The air is thick. Now it swirls.

It isn't air.

As in the *Iliad*,
death is continually swirling over
the bravest warriors from its source
in some tornado cellar or storage bin of death
and never in a straight line—as though it were embarrassed
to be seen for what it is and chose
the devious route. Not that
it can't directly target those whom it
chooses, but that it chooses not to.

A roughly trapezoidal shadow
has swirled up the side of the building opposite,
making its sooty brick facing darker than normally.
Some cars emerge from its insides.

One is making a left turn
from the extreme right lane.

CHARLES NORTH

When you think of the
truly instinctual moments, crying out
when the door slams on your foot,
or breathing deeply of spring, it seems only natural
to imagine an opposite way of behaving.

And when instinct is visible,
as clear in the air as leaves and water tanks,
it isn't inconceivable to suppose
an infinite number of possible worlds, bargained for, grasped,
and finally let go at the moment the situation
becomes clear, like storm clouds illuminating a herd of cows
nestled against coal-black tree trunks—*n'est-ce pas*?

And in composing for wind instruments
and putting the same or nearly the same chords
into two different pieces, you are
not likely to hear the same concert at noon
as at dusk—unless, of course, the performances are all illusion
and those in attendance merely marking time
within their own private band shells.

Certo.

An example of feeling
not quite taking the place of thought,
although memorized by it.

The house I live in.
The block of wood and the wood chips,

the surrounding proof that things exist outside the self
despite constant weeding. A waterfall of selves.

The mice are a nice touch, they don't have to speak in complete
    sentences.
Also the sawhorses.
One, sprinkled with life force,
took off a few minutes ago. Stung by its freedom,
whirling to gain a sense of direction,
it hovered over New Jersey for several seconds
before making a U-turn.

No, you turn.

Does the name R. Penis Blavatsky mean anything, at all, to you?

Personally, I think
you need to focus on what is really important to you: change
habits as well as clothes. The shadows
that fall on wet rooftops altering them irrevocably,
new notions in hospital architecture,
half-built buildings with their shirt-sleeved inhabitants
in Italian movies of the sixties, etc.

You, with the neck that moved.
No, *you*; the shadows making their way
inside the paperweight, diffusing the glare that falls on
    upturned palm,
chin, cheek, even the occasional glancing blow
branching off into language.

Here you are a highly educated person. Hands, feet, chin,
    everything.
One morning, out of the blue,
a flock of wild turkeys
paraded up the hill from the road, at least forty
by actual count. The oddest thing was
their landing on the grass in small squads,
one at a time, with a parent figure
at either end, to march
steadily and without concern
for conceivably life-threatening surroundings
—in sharp contrast to the high-strung and
hyperactive deer—and just as suddenly
vanish into the mix of cedars and dark green shadows.

Here you resemble an aquamanile, your notions poached in
    rainwater.

Devoted dentist, darling chirurgeon, beloved branch manager,
dear critic, fragrant disciple,
esteemed concert mistress, caring strip miner,
wondrous instantiater, affectionate florist, moving engineer,
imaginative groundskeeper, tender restaurateur,
desirable glazier, charismatic coroner,
self-abnegating occultist, glowing restorer, lissome umpire...

Paper-thin traces of Being with needles sticking out of some but
    not all of them...

You, for example,

could be the Allegorical Figure of Taxation;

but more (I hope) about that later.

As Dizzy Gillespie is, or was, the god of the winds.

I am at a college interview. Each

of the interviewers is simultaneously

being interviewed. While she fields questions from all sides,

my interviewer shouts questions at me

from the far end of a long refectory table. I can

barely hear her over the din

but find myself admiring the way she responds to

those questions aimed directly at her. Then

I am face to face with someone who

asks if I prefer cloth- or paperbound books; but

just as I am about to respond he takes a wooden spoon

and flings some hard, uncooked grains of oatmeal towards the
  ceiling

where they hang suspended in the air

like a display of space matter in a planetarium.

Is that lighter—or just grayer?

In fact, for a long time

I've felt like apologizing

for what seem to me excessive references to darkness

as though the available light were on trial.

Sometimes it's virtually impossible

to get up in the morning. The days in
the middle of winter when it doesn't begin
to get light till 7 a.m. or even later,
the swirl commandeering hydrants, curbstones,
stoops, etc. To brush back shadows
from the cheek of night. "To be,"
as Thomas Browne wrote, "a kind of nothing
for a moment," a balloon with a beard...

Meanwhile, the cows on the postcard from the college bookstore
have moved from in front of a clump
of shade trees to somewhere more virtual. Peasants
looking stoned, lying face up underneath a table groaning with
   food,
searching the invisible sky as well as each other
for clues regarding their current state: one of
pleasant stupor, or stupefied fullness,
as symbolized in the dazed-looking
small game and surreal life forms attending the postmortem
of what has clearly been a positive experience
for most of them—although not without a trace of some
prior violence, most obviously in long broken cudgels
but also in a branch bent like a catapult
and in the dizzying angle, everything
about to topple into the whirlpool or quicksand of satisfaction
inside which a pipe can tip over a table. (*Das Schlaraffenland*,
   1567)

Not exactly pleasant
but not entirely unpleasant either.

Somewhat like "turning
over in your grave." The breeze tingling.

I don't think the subject has changed significantly.

I'm thinking of a noun,
any noun. I picture it
as hard rubber, darkly resinous,
the same family, roughly speaking, as Being-in-Itself.

Each of the slots can be and is filled
by a person, place, thing
or other suitable substantive.

Currently the slots come with appropriate hat sizes,
5½ being one of the most popular (Beauty in itself
being rather stupid, in case you haven't already noticed).

While you were painting
the rather severe downpour stopped.
Slowed first, to avoid jolting
the already battered air conditioners.
I don't know about you
but I frequently have the feeling
that the buildings are mere skin, bruised by dusk,
little by little powerless to do
more than ripple, comparable to the rippling that erupts out of
    flatness
to be rolled out and attenuated like the most attenuated

of clouds. What moments are to
themselves: not so much moving as scaffolding.

How do you *know*
or can you *prove*
that the evening doesn't subsist on pure will—
short and fat, thick-necked,
wheezing like a woodchuck, its inner
life a barrel vault, clinging to the last chord played,
the last note written?

In Smokey Joe's Cafe.

To put it in epic terms—Thinkology
but once removed. How anyone comes to live in
a world of oxbows, steppes, wheat fields, and projective versts.

For you are the electronic type: your keys are oxblood and
    celadon stars.

I see, or am beginning to,
that your reliance on night is genuflectory.
But so do the dark references
resemble life: life after death.
How

it is possible
and also impossible to be the imagination
of a future time. Which is to say that,
given a little more time,

the consequences for both city and rural life
can and must distinguish themselves—unlike the beauties of New
  Hampshire
arm in arm with the beauties of Vermont.

A ball of frosted light
just whirled over the Hudson,
coming to rest on a lamppost. Which
bats it to another. The maroon
of a coffee shop awning utterly divorced from
its lower extenders, barely visible, like the bouffant of an
  angel

or as Dorothy Wordsworth reported
of an especially beautiful May afternoon, "I drank
a little Brandy and water, and was in heaven."

Clearly not the same as
landing in the middle of Herald Square
wearing Valkyrie gear and dancing a pavanne
to celebrate the sudden change in seasons.

Still,
comparison to the other arts seems
all but inevitable, as witness the so-called
Clarinetist's Fallacy, coaxing excessive
feeling out of what is essentially a cold instrument
if brilliantly so—the result being a whining
masquerading as feeling

whereas the best playing is "cold and passionate
as the dawn."

"The reed is held on the mouthpiece
by a soft rubber support which has sluts.
A very pure dound is obstained by an metallic plate
mounled directly behind of the rubber support.
The whole device is in the form of a flexible band very
　　resistant
adjusted by two screws, to allow adjustment for personal
　　playing styles...

　　—casy sound production
　　—a very rich sounding note
　　—a naturally obstained pure sound.

　　A/Remove the adjusting screurs
　　B/Place the reed on the mathpiece
C/Carefully position the ligature around the mountpiece
　　plus reed
　　D/Fit the crews and tighten..." [sic]

Foghorns in the atmosphere
of Smokey Joe's Café. In
or just behind it, in an alleyway
lined with stucco and graffiti from the sixties.

As the life force plays tricks
plus the two Brahms Sonatas for clarinet (or viola) and piano.

CHARLES NORTH   47

Some whiteness is beginning
to show around the edges
but not in all places at once.
The bills have been paid; Mozart
is playing quietly in the background
aged 2½; a few of the dark clumps, wads of emptiness,
anchor the deer and the echoing cedars. A few
more particles than usual: to put aside, focus on, or just
chuck out never and nowhere to be witnessed again ever.

Your lids are getting heavy.
People carrying water faucets keep attempting to put you out.

North of the Charles...

My name,
actually my middle name, is Alphonse
and I live in northern Alberta,
but have a summer palace near Albuquerque.
Of adobe. Behind the brickwork.

The close colors depart in droves.

To write
          a nation or thriving city-state.
The Queen Anne's Lace
                    dove in.

Meanwhile, deer consumption
—by and not of—

has proceeded at a fairly alarming rate.
Nearing the surface they chin upwards
slicing the air into deer and not-deer. Pruning
to within an inch of life, which in this case
happens to read as broad daylight
despite a charcoal gray fuzz directly overhead
like a sweater on a minaret.

You have received a grant to do hornet work...
standing on your head
not to mention endless attention to the shivers
that erupt. There was a just stained look to the sky
that lasted most of the morning, leaving
rags at the edges. Not merely cloud shreds
or broccoli-covered cliffs; the perforations
through which the breeze enters like woodwinds: the bright
    glow of new leaves
magnetizing unspeakably charged states of being.

Just before dusk,
a whole notebookful of sense impressions flitted around
the trunk of a maple tree,
a fairly young one,
looking for a hole in the protective wrapping.

A woman in a cream-colored blouse and blue apron
bends at a 90° angle to fill a lustrous pitcher from a copper-
    colored urn.
Leaning out the window the evening clouds floated by.

STUDY FOR "DAY AFTER DAY THE STORM MOUNTED. THEN IT DISMOUNTED"

Devoted dentist, darling chirurgeon, beloved mailman,
dear critic, fragrant disciple,
esteemed second violinist, caring strip miner,
delightful bagman, wondrous instantiater,
affectionate florist, moving engineer, embraceable barber,
imaginative umpire, tender restaurateur,
desirable glazier, lissome dwarf, humble go-getter,
self-abnegating groundskeeper, glowing restorer, tender agent,
ravishing dunner, adored kayaker,
considerate bathing beauty, warm slam-dunker, delicate rabbi,
undisgruntled grant applier, tasteful chastiser,
huggable frontier scout, kind futurist, lively thief,
haunting numismatist, glistening bartender,
full-breasted chairperson, melting dealer, translucent branch
    manager,
angelic burgomaster, generous do-it-yourselfer,
herniating operatic tenor, congenial wide receiver,
exemplary bailiff, stimulating mobster, cute rum-runner,
willowy executionist, life-promoting tour guide,
handy antagonist, caressed misprizer,
cherished inkeeper, head-turning pharmacist,
ached-for sous chef, unforgettable fogie, seductive pointillist,
riveting sophist, missed beadle, magnetic muezzin,
well-meaning bowler, dedicated phrenologist,
precious typist, seraphic song stylist, winsome CEO,
idolized quick study, dearly beloved test pilot,
undetested laundress, pet decoder, lovesome party leader

CHARLES NORTH

TRANSLATION

I feel you very close to me
In the same way that sky and air seem not two things but one
Those termite-like pests are attacking the two-by-fours
O two-by-fours

In the same way that sky and air seem not two things but one
The small elevations eventually touch
O two-by-fours
Masked like cattle with cutouts of sun glued to them

The small elevations eventually touch
All they are allotted in the way of dull urban skies
Masked like cattle with cutouts of sun glued to them
To make a long story short we need extricating

All they are allotted in the way of dull urban skies
The streams on the map lend something of themselves
To make a long story short we need extricating
Though that doesn't hold a candle to out-and-out mental disarray

The streams on the map lend something of themselves
Periodically rising above the longing
Though that doesn't hold a candle to out-and-out mental disarray
With one exception: it puts an end to usual ways of speaking and
    behaving

Periodically rising above the longing
My poem to you is difficult to pin down

With one exception: it puts an end to usual ways of speaking and
   behaving
Like October entering earth's atmosphere in flames

SUMMER OF LIVING DANGEROUSLY

June 16. Sun then no sun then sun then no sun for the foreseeable future.

June 20. The species have the life.

June 22. Listening to the Mozart Clarinet Concerto on the radio with the A.C. on and they play it all the way through. Not that an isolated movement can't be enjoyable in spite of oneself. Competent and more but not as good as it should be—he muttered, after not having played it through cleanly for years! Actually, I was pretty sure I knew who it was right from the start, tonguing if anything *too* fast, a little show-offy, even some roughness in fast passages.

Faster than the wild turkeys who clearly know where their safe havens lie and make a beeline for them regardless of who notices, their collars graven round about.

So who was it.

June 24. A tiny—though probably not as tiny as it looked from where I was sitting—brown bird hung in the air like a hummingbird then shot off while others were busy exploring below. Downwind of roses.

The pair of cardinals that zip around like flying drops of blood... let's make that like ice-dancers, especially when compared to the deliberate hawks. The latter have a continuous relationship but a continually shifting one, so that a straight line connecting them at any given moment is one of an infinite number of variables. Neither is what we mean by chaos, but each has a somewhat unsettling if partly pleasing randomness. A blood bank of cardinals. A plane geometry of hawks.

A throwback of oafs. An Assignment of Poems (for KK).

June 25. Rainy and esoteric.

June 26. Light rain with a thick border of drizzle.

June 29. We don't ordinarily think of clouds as minds, but they exhibit some of the same forms of detachment, from "spacing out" to "scattering" to disintegration. Plus the appearance at least of being superimposed, more convincingly at certain times than at others.

July 1. Stammering.

July 3. Stammering until after dark.

July 5. How about coming back as a *bad* poet or a *bad* painter?

The turn in English cattle-breeding (domesticated animals generally) comes in the mid-18th century with the so-called improvements—the Cardboard Bull with the piercing eye and internal organs worn on its hide; the Heartbreaking White Ram with the second "ram" clinging to its underside; legions of horses, chickens and pigs, and notably the Improved Suffolk

Pig (painted in 1862 by the prolific animal portraitist John Vine as a thoughtful duffel bag) and the 802-lb. Spherical Pig, which lived to the age of 2½, a tragic football inflated for prizes (painted and later engraved after the painting), its tiny trotters far too small and glued on to hold up its colossal body.

July 6. Dark again, wet, a little screwy in the topgallants, meaning... not very.

This is how the schedule is shaping up:

Uglification
Writing off
Gladly yearning & gladly leaching
Hegemony
Pseudopoetics
Breast period
Abscess
Colonization
Higher myth

It isn't written in stone.

July 8. King Lear walks into a bar. Why the subdivision?

July 10. Trying to get hot, trying to get cool, trying to appear nonchalant but not fumblingly as in *sprezzatura*, which is clearly over-rated—at least once you make it out of your teens, which this summer clearly has.

July 11. Méséglise drops: "Never drifting apart, never wandering off on their own during their rapid course, but each one keeping its place and drawing its successor in its wake."

July 15 (for John Ashbery). The factory, which was a 6-floor building in the garment district, lasted for about a decade, and then only because the authorities were paid to look the other way. It wasn't all fangs and blood, but there were a lot of tie-ins. The female employees were named Velma. I worked one summer as their elevator operator, and was amazed at what you can get used to. Not that I was exactly thrilled by my wolf costume—nor did anyone appear to care much about the inevitable confusions between worker and product. There was something both exalted and exalting about the absolute stillness and high blue sky underneath which the wolves stood at strict attention, just before the whistle blew for lunch.

July 19. The same late afternoon clouds, I swear, as yesterday—unlike the cow dung the philosopher Heraclitus lay down in, in legend and apparently also in fact, in order to cure his dropsy, only to be eaten by a pack of wild dogs who evidently found the combination too enticing to circumvent twice.

July 22. How about brown light through a rose window, there's your wine-dark sea.

—I did that already.

Socks made of wool
facing feet made of sheep.

Hogs report to shingled roof. On the double.

Make room.

July 28. Suppose the dreams are getting advices, what does "advice"
    mean. Suppose it means I advise you to read this and hope
    very much that you will be able to do so.

July 29. The rain finally came and finally left. In between, steady
    downpour followed by incredible, which is to say, computer-
    generated, fog—strands, fronds, wall hangings, tarpaulins,
    dark disdain—rising from below ground and threatening to
    foreclose on air. It thinned out a little on the open highway,
    only to gather elsewhere with a lumpish vengeance. The tiny
    white toads flopping across the winding lane by the pond
    seemed as terrified as the fleeing deer in *Bambi*, but for all
    anyone knows they could have been enjoying themselves, like a
    dog that gets a chance to let loose after being cooped up in an
    apartment all day.

Unmannerly threats, the chess champion Reuben Fine, adipose
    tissue,
  Dvorak's *Humoresque*

July 30. A Hunt Cantata of clouds.

Aug. 1. Interesting that "petrified" means extreme fright when in
    reality both fight and flight involve extremes of action rather
    than being turned to stone. Hearts made of stone. Too long a
    sacrifice can make a stone of the heart. Is that, the paralysis

factor, what was going on with the Medusa, shutdown of the autonomic nervous system, coma so to speak of everything in sight?

I keep staring at the space underneath a large—sycamore tree
    it looks like, darker than one would imagine even in bad
    weather. Than I would have imagined.

Well, stop.

Aug. 2. A water pipe crawled out of the woods.

Aug. 4. I am in front of a large college audience about to give my
    opening Charles Eliot North Lecture, but before I can utter
    a word someone asks a question and I spend the entire time
    trying to answer it. I have something written on a paper on
    top of the lectern, but I've never seen the paper before and the
    writing doesn't look like English. When the allotted time is up
    I get some seemingly genuine applause. The wall at my back is
    all glass. Behind it is a "planned miniature forest" built for the
    occasion, into which everyone rushes the second the applause
    stops.

Aug. 5. Ceci n'est pas un diary.

Aug. 6. A pretty good morning: clear, well-defined clouds; no over-
    reaching. Towards mid-day less well-defined so the reach was
    ambiguous—ultimately prophetic as it darkened uncontrollably
    and began to pour and never stopped. So: an alert start,

followed by a short but emblematic gray area, and a largely bitter, peaty finish.

Aug 9–13. Stammering.

Aug. 14. The *pas moi*. And what, exactly, do I mean by that.

I mean it shows.

(P.M.) Thirty or so of the neighborhood turkeys poking down the hill; rest period underneath the cedars; loud thunderclap; some rain; names not as rigid but rigid enough; sun a hero but so are the simulacra, one with a yarmulke and playing Klezmer clarinet; you with the raptness emblazoned; wave function denied access so it pops up elsewhere, like Chopin in the 20th century; November till noon; oscillations of October; art and the trucks; Liszt at the Kit Kat Club.

Aug. 19. This Netting-and-Thug Capital I keep trying to write about is beginning to seem like a theme park rather than a hospital... though clearly the thugs have little if anything to do. Mostly they just stand around as though on an endless coffee break. Could they conceivably be taking part in some unannounced job action? Most likely they have simply ceased to function in the manner to which I am accustomed, which brings up the interesting issue of when they stop being thugs and have to be called by some other name.

On the other hand and perhaps more to the point, the netting is *too* palpable, all cords and no interstices, like a crawl space whose floorboards are nowhere and whose low ceiling is everywhere.

Aug. 21. I heard a deer *honk* when I woke up. Quietly so as not to wake anyone else.

Aug. 24. A long line of vehicles, from 18-wheelers to mountain bikes and those silver scooters that were so popular a couple of years ago, stacked up in front of a rural railroad crossing, ridge of foothills in the distance. Two large heavyset men in dark business suits and white socks, pants a little too short, lying on their sides on the grass intent on fixing something at track level.

The postcard version of life gets an unnecessarily bad rap. It's one among many, not necessarily false or reductive. To say it distorts the *tone* of life is to describe in a realistic manner an aspect of life that is as real as any other.

Aug. 25. Rain promised again—strange sort of promise—but zilch so far (mid-afternoon). Whole blocks of sky moving slowly as if painfully, or as if hiding something that would be painful if revealed.

Just before dusk a strip of bluish acetate like the thin wash of clouds the saints go marching in.

Aug. 29. IMPOSTERS BLAST PERPS!

Actually I'm almost positive it's impasto, and probably turps as
     well, as in artists' turpentine, so painting is somewhere close
     by if not in the apartment this second. What is here are the
     baboons, who have waited patiently for their *babooneries,* put
     their right paws in, take them out, put them in again, shake
     them, and spatter paint over the sidewalk, the open hydrant,
     the parked cars, the lamppost bases, the first-floor window
     panes and –guards, as well as their own colorful smocks and
     neatly organized palettes.

Sept. 2. Grisaille.

Sept. 4. Life being serially monogamous.

Sept. 8. Dark dark dark, then a hint of blue, then the sky which
     had been working hard all day to get clear finally did so. A
     blue-collar day, but with some elegance (Dave Debusschere—
     though arguably the whole of the 1970–73 Knicks).

Sept. 12. Air sweetened by foreheads.

Sept. 13. Music from somewhere below, too far away to distinguish.
     For some reason the name "Morpeth Rant" came to mind—is
     that, as I dimly (probably inaccurately) recall, an old ballad
     which I used to play when I was a beginner? Could it be,
     though I don't know what it would mean, "Morpeth Rath"?
     Possibly an English town? A path across a moor? I can't
     imagine it's "Wrath"—unless it has something to do with a
     fight or battle, which is possible: Sing, goddess, of the wrath of
     _____. Not that rant and wrath are so different.

Sept. 14. What am I a lyre or a sink.

Late afternoon shafts of freckled gold like alto sax reeds. With a
green matte varnish.

The dark is boyish when you think about it.

Sept. 17. I'm struck, as I'm sure others are, by the "shalt" in
Donne's "Death thou shalt die" sonnet. A lot more than by
Dylan Thomas's (hardly read any more is my guess) "And
death shall have no dominion." The imperative mood attached
to the future tense, i.e., wish as much as forecast. A wishful
forecast. There *will be* no more dying. *Then.*

Let me know.

Sept. 18. Speaking of scattering, isn't there a rhetorical term for
loosening a word from its proper object and letting it drift to
something that's merely in the vicinity? Allen Ginsberg does
it in "Howl" as do a lot of others. Looking for an angry fix. O
moon with how sad steps thou climb'st the sky.

The line stretching between the two Hotels de Ville across
Broadway was visible for a few minutes early this morning—a
thin, fleeting metonymy. How come air conditioners, vacuums,
major appliances, etc., aren't given seductive names like cars?
The Fedders Igloo. The Friedrich Zero Tolerance. Electrolux
Suck-Up.

Oxford UP has *The Philosophy of Avenues* slated for fall 2005 or spring 2006.

Sept. 20–22. Obsessive-compulsive humidity.

Sept. 25. The ghost of a day. Partly rainy. Partly sunny. Partly not there.

Sept. 26. A colorful morning inside a lucite frame. The autumn of the highway thrown in for effect, but the effect is mixed: ground down like incisors, already some chipping and resurfacing, occasional uprooting followed by wholesale restoration, bridgework, new posts, etc. The day that started out as though it would be bright and pleasantly breezy, even a little chilly for September, but fell in with bad company and wound up deteriorating in just about every sense, including the spiritual, isn't a rigid designator.

Sept. 28. The following are rigid designators: Johnny Vander Meer, Johnny Friendly, Peter Unger, Marjorie Perloff, The Man That Corrupted Hadleyburg, the Widow Wadman, Ralph Waldo Emerson, Julie Schwarz, Ken Schwarz, the Sears Tower. The man who wrote *Seven Types of Ambiguity* isn't a rigid designator, as there is nothing necessary about his having written that book, or about the fact that what he did write had that name, or even that he was a critic in addition to being a poet. We can imagine possible worlds where he taught shop or raced Formula 1 automobiles. The notion of rigid designator is intuitively satisfying and "stood analytic philosophy on its ear," as one of the blurbs on the back of Saul Kripke's landmark *Naming and Necessity* attests. Yet the man who wrote *Naming and Necessity* isn't a rigid designator, nor is the man who presented the substantial text of what would become the book at Princeton in a series of three lectures (with no notes) over a period of just over a week in January 1970, which for its importance rivals (if it doesn't exceed) Allen Ginsberg's reading of "Howl" in 1955. Yet exciting as those three evenings must have been for the philosophy community and the history of ideas in general, the use of a rigid designator for something or someone who no longer exists brings with it a poignancy that can sometimes verge on the intolerable, and that amounts, at least arguably, to designating a (rigid) designator, i.e., something that formerly referred in a rigid way to the same person in all possible worlds but now refers, in a far paler way, to a cluster of qualities, appearance, life's work, etc., that exists only in or as memory. That is to say, we continue to use the designation—or pretend to use it, though with no pejoratives attaching to pretend—in the same way even though, rather than being the same reference, it is somehow cut off before it has a chance to travel very far—I would go so far as to suggest, before it has a chance to really get started—hence really more of a stammer than a reference, or else a stammered reference, the non-referential aspect becoming progressively clear as well as progressively poignant over time. Rather than having its meaning or meaningfulness in some counterfactual world, it resides wholly in this one whereas the person designated no longer does, the gap between the two being such as to be progressively intolerable. It isn't, that is to say, like either Johnny Friendly or Remedios the Beauty, but rather like Robert Campin or Jacqueline du Pré.

Sept. 30. It isn't as though the designation itself is any less
rigid (there are no other candidates for the object of the
designation) but that what is designated is "different from
what it was before it changed," as Thomas Hardy would put it,
in the possible, i.e., logical, worlds in which it formerly had its
meaning. Nor is it a mental shorthand. And yet we continue to
use it (or pretend to use it) in the same way, even though the
reference itself is cut off almost before it has a chance to get
started, so that it is really more of a stammer than a reference,
a stammered reference, the non-referential aspect becoming
clearer as well as increasingly poignant as time passes.

PAIN QUOTIENT

for David Watson

1.

How to explain tragedy to a deer. This is the assignment.—Well,
it isn't the assignment it's in the general category of things
assigned, like growing to a mature height of four inches if you
happen to be a certain strain of ornamental cactus, or being
shamed back to life by any means possible. I like the idea that
hope springs eternal, especially as the adjective, not adverb
suggests that spring is a verb of being rather than action, it
doesn't have to be imagined or looked forward to, or yearned
for, or original in any sense of the word. The present which is
always with us, regardless. Take the piano music of objects,
the black-and-white, the mystical harmonics, bipolarities, etc.

2.

The afternoon smells like rosemary, whereas the morning was on
the visual side, jutting among the albums. Someone David
knew, an actress, referred to the café Pain Quotidien as Pain
Quotient, apparently with a straight face. *The Daily Pain*
(which I seem to remember my father bringing home from
work). Or if you happen to be in show business, the pan. Take
the extremist willows.

3.

5:30 p.m. The soul goes out for its walk—just be sure you're back
in time for supper. The colors look pasted on, washy blue like

a robin's egg seen through a landlord shade, then just washed
away. Where is conceptual art when you need it. Everyone
knows that Janus Weathercock and Cornelius Van Vinckboons
are too good not to be true, but very few know of their
connection to the poet John Clare. Or that "they" were in fact
the same person, who not only worked for *London Magazine*
in the early part of the 19th century but was, according to
Clare's biographer Jonathan Bate, "the Oscar Wilde of his
day." I say metaphors have it easy! Brahms surging, receding,
churning the already churned foam of Being
whereas Rachmaninov is like a fist to the heart.

4.

Suppose everyone were a lot less talkative. Or were prohibited
from talking to anyone who spoke the same language, not
only people but houseplants, raccoons, self-service elevators,
winged salesmen from the future, etc. A gem-like solid framed
by a ribbon of aluminum light. Begins in speech but is diverted
primarily by all the mistakes from the remembered past.
Another episode has a word whirling around its phonemes
which are also whirling. We were talking about shaming
someone back into life, the blood verities. Hanging in the air
"like a memory lost" but recapturable if you don't mind the
mix of truth and sprawl, fragments of all that can be thought
without accompaniment or fixation. Or *whatness*. The star
drawer helps with the street noise. Lines, half-lines, whorls,
turquoise, i.e., green mixed with blue, highlights. Characters
get dragged in kicking and screaming from the wings and
forget their resonant ties to objects. To be calmer than a rug,
a particle from the 1940s, dizzying, I'll take it. But you can

have the stifling dream states, like a perpetual air-raid. Why so many notions settling in the middle of the forehead like a *tableau vivant*—so much more cause than affect. The summer retired early; was forced out, actually, like the recorder family from mainstream music. Mixed-use but heartfelt skyline.

LIFE

Photo Credit: Unknown

Charles North is a distinguished-looking man with a gentle face, slender build, longish gray hair, and sharp blue eyes that radiate kindness and intellect behind dark-rimmed glasses. He loves music, painting, movies, and sports; enjoys eating, drinks wine and an occasional whiskey; and lives a fairly scheduled life between teaching, writing, and family. From his younger days through middle adulthood, he was quite shy among people he didn't know well but feels he is a lot more open these days. During the bulk of our conversations, he sat attentively on a sun-faded couch in the living room of the spacious Upper West Side apartment he shares with his wife of 50 years, the painter Paula North. Paula and he have a warm, admiring relationship and he rarely attends poetry events or dinner parties without her. They have also collaborated through the years artistically. For example, his work Complete Lineups *(2008) was published with a cover, drawings, and reproductions of artwork by Paula, and The Song Cave recently brought out* Translation, *his chapbook "translating" five of his own poems into English, with covers and drawings by* Paula. *Their rent-regulated apartment has the warm, bohemian feel of dusty books, musical instruments (clarinets, recorders, a saxophone, a guitar, a tiny baby grand piano), and comfortable, overstuffed chairs and couch. It is also full of Paula's oil portraits, still-lifes, and landscapes, as well as artworks by painter friends like Trevor Winkfield and Rackstraw Downes. Two of the portraits (one by Louise Hamlin from the mid-'80s) are of Charles in his late 30s and early 40s. His hair is brown, more plentiful, and longer, but otherwise he looks the same.*

EARLY HISTORY

Sometimes I think I'm
close to discovering
why half my life has occurred
in a fog, which makes
the other half radiant
by comparison.

—from "A Note On Labor Day" (1989)

CHARLES LAURENCE NORTH was born in 1941 in Brooklyn to Jewish-American parents, Russian on both sides. His father attended Townsend Harris, one of the best high schools in the city, went to work at 15, took accounting courses at CCNY, and eventually earned two law degrees from Brooklyn College, attending classes at night. He worked in the textile business in Manhattan, and the family moved to Manhattan just after Charles' birth. His only sibling, his sister Julie, was born three years later in 1944. In 1950, the upwardly mobile family moved to the then-rural suburbs of Westchester County.

His mother came from a middle-class household that placed great value on literature and music. Her father owned a cigar store and was an opera buff who walked long distances to performances. She studied piano and before Charles was born worked as a journalist, writing a travel column for *The Brooklyn Eagle* (which, incidentally, was edited a century earlier by Walt Whitman) and ghostwriting speeches and other prose for business people. She was also something of a fiction writer manqué, and Charles recalls hearing about her unsuccessful attempts to publish both adult and children's fiction. As a grade-schooler, Charles won several local prose-writing competitions. He briefly tried fiction in college and was excited to have a story he wrote in his freshman English class (the same class where he met his wife, Paula) published in the college literary magazine. But he had no serious thoughts about becoming a writer until his middle twenties, and at that point was drawn more to poetry than prose.

Music permeated the North household and had an abiding influence on both children, as did their parents' love of books. Charles recalls playing with toys in his pre-school years near the family piano while his mother regularly practiced. When he was ten, somewhat by chance—since a family friend knew someone who taught clarinet—Charles began to study clarinet and soon excelled. (His sister is also very musical and has performed, written, and recorded music.) At the age of thirteen he shyly auditioned for the semi-professional Westchester Symphony Orchestra and became part of the group. In 1955 he spent the first of three summers at the National Music Camp in Interlochen, Michigan, where he studied with a Chicago Symphony clarinetist and gradually worked his way to the upper echelon of the young clarinetists, several of whom went on to play with major U.S. orchestras.

Despite his talent, he decided against a career in music. To his parents, who had lived through the Great Depression on little income, a career meant something secure like law or medicine, and they discouraged him from music. Moreover, he had trouble taking his success as seriously as others did, and although he performed a good deal during his high school years—all-state and all-county (first chair) concert bands, local orchestras, chamber music as well as solo performances—it was almost always accompanied by anxiety. Charles confesses to being haunted even now by "occasionally overwhelming nostalgia" for his musical life as a teenager. Given the fact that playing music was his primary source of emotional expression, he was cut off from a vital source of life and creativity at a formative age. Perhaps not surprisingly, clarinets appear as a recurring trope in his poetry; he even uses the word "haunting" in a poem titled "Clarinet"

(1987), an adaptation of the 18th-century French poet André Chénier's short rhyming poem "La Flute":

> Less than a recurrent dream, but more haunting.
> The clarinet is poised and I begin playing,
> conscious of occupying some exact center
> where I am both rival and conqueror.
> My usually awkward embouchure
> produces tones which are inspired and pure.

His embouchure is able to produce "tones which are inspired and pure." Embouchure refers to the use of facial muscles and shaping of the lips to the mouthpieces of woodwind and brass instruments. A proper embouchure enables an instrumentalist to play his instrument at its full range without strain or damage to the oral muscles. Other references to the clarinet can be found in the poems "Some Versions of Reeds" (1974), "Day After Day the Storm Mounted, Then It Dismounted" (2000), and "Summer of Living Dangerously" (2007), only to name a few.

Although Charles speaks appreciatively of his mother's musical influence and her "drumming grammar and proper sentence structure" into him, and his father's sharp mind, his feelings towards his parents are complicated. Both he and his younger sister endured a mother and father who were, as he puts it, "inadequate as parents, in both standard and creative ways, for a variety of reasons having to do with their own emotional problems." Early childhood he remembers as a mostly gloomy time; even the memories of his mother playing at the piano are tinged with sadness. Looking back, Charles is surprised by just how much of his childhood he seems to have blocked out. He does, however, have fond memories of playing in Central Park as a young child before moving north to Westchester in 1950:

I grew up on 96th Street, just off Columbus Avenue, just a block away from Central Park. And the school I went to was even a little bit closer to the park, and I went there on weekends. Some of the happiest times I remember were running around and playing baseball and tag and everything else in the park. So much so that the smell of nature to me always has the smell of the ground in Central Park, and the horse shit on the bridal path; it really was very important to me, until I turned nine and we moved north to Westchester.

The outdoors continued to mean a lot after his family's move:

When my parents moved to what's now the suburbs, it was pretty rural: a lot of undeveloped land, a lot of woods; so after the age of nine it was still really the country. There were some deer, and woods, fields, and air, and I frequently walked home from school, which was a mile and a half. This was 1950, when people who could newly afford it were beginning to move out of the city.

He also has fond memories of the time he spent as a young child with his mother at the local branch of the New York Public Library. He loved returning home with a pile of borrowed books, especially on mythology, or even more exciting, the library books that were occasionally on sale for a dime or quarter. These memories aside, Charles had a hard time responding when asked whether his childhood was a happy time:

I know it's a natural question and the response ought to be yes, but I'm not sure what the response really is. Really, I'm not sure whether I was unhappier or happier than I was, say, in high school.

Although he describes feeling "wiped out" by adolescence, his high school years were outwardly quite positive. He had many friends, including girlfriends, was a leader of a number organizations including the high school newspaper, played sax in a dance band, and lettered in track. No one seemed to catch on that underneath he often felt nervous and depressed. Sports were a great outlet. "My recollection is that just about every day of my life after school, depending on what season it was, I was out shooting basketballs, or playing baseball, football or tennis, or running sprints." In response to a question about early romance, he mentions being "stood up" for the only time in his life by a Canadian girl—whom he remembers as "dark-haired and pretty, probably an early Paula"—he had made a date with towards the close of one summer at Interlochen. He still remembers how surprised and hurt he was.

Charles enrolled, "with a chip on [his] shoulder," at Tufts University in 1958 soon after he turned 17. He had been the top-ranked boy in his class—receiving the math award at graduation—and was advised that he didn't need to apply to a "safety school"; nonetheless, he was wait-listed at Harvard, Amherst, and Brown, which devastated him. In June of his senior year his Dean phoned Tufts, to which Charles had not applied, and managed to get him an interview; he was immediately accepted. Although he had to take a room off campus for his first semester and for a time was set on transferring, the silver lining, apart from discovering a charismatic English professor, Sylvan Barnet, who became his advisor, and a philosophy professor who stimulated a lifelong interest in philosophy, was meeting his future wife, Paula. She was a student in the first English class he took. He describes being immediately attracted to her, but couldn't work up the nerve to ask her on a date until midway through their sophomore year. Their first date was a reading given on campus by

Robert Frost. Charles recalls that Frost was unpleasant during the reading and snapped at someone in the audience who may have been opening a candy wrapper.

Charles double-majored in English and philosophy (and effectively minored in French), and after graduating began a Master's program in English at Columbia University. At that point he had no particular interest in poetry. Paula and he moved to Manhattan separately, and then were married in June 1963.

After finishing his coursework at Columbia, though not his Master's thesis, he decided not to go on for the Ph.D. Not knowing what he wanted to do, he followed in the footsteps of a college friend who had gone on from English studies at Columbia to law school. In Charles' case, it was Harvard, which pleased his father tremendously; not only was it a top law school, but the degree promised to open many career doors. Paula and he moved to Cambridge as husband and wife, and Charles spent the summer in Widener Library trying to finish his Master's thesis. The association with Harvard, though, turned out to be short-lived. Charles describes a rapid realization that law was not for him; he officially withdrew only six weeks into the term but stopped going to classes before that. He recalls the Law School Dean informing him that, of those who did drop out, virtually all did so as early as he. The most difficult part of the decision was his knowing how much it would disappoint his parents, to whom he sent a letter explaining why. When I nudged him to say more about how they (particularly his father) responded to the letter, he sent me the following email from his office at Pace University:

> This is a difficult one. First, I don't really remember the letter—no doubt blocked out the experience—and second, I do feel this is on the private side. I know I was aware that

my parents would be disappointed, but don't know what else I can say. The most important thing is that I knew almost instantly that the law wasn't for me. At the time I didn't know I wanted to write poetry; but—with apologies for the hint of "depth psychology"—I'm sure something was simmering underneath.

The Norths stayed in Cambridge for the rest of the school year, Charles finishing his thesis (he was awarded the degree in 1964) and Paula working, rather unhappily, as a secretary at M.I.T. for an autocratic Nobel-Prize-winning physicist. Once again uncertain about what to do next, he applied and was accepted to a Ph.D. program in philosophy at Columbia with a plan to concentrate on aesthetics, but never enrolled. Instead, the Norths sold their car, scraped together some money from savings, borrowed some more, and traveled to Europe—briefly to London, then Paris for six months, then Antibes—where it was possible then to live very cheaply.

In Paris they sublet an apartment on the Left Bank near the Boulevard St. Germain and enjoyed the time immensely. They walked around the city and frequently went to art museums and galleries, as well as to the Cinémathèque and the many tiny movie houses that showed old movies at discount prices for those with student cards. At one point Charles thought about a program in film studies. Paula, who had displayed her artistic talent from an early age, painted in the living room of their apartment, and for a time took classes at the Académie de la Grande Chaumière. Charles spent much time reading and attempting to write, mostly fiction. One of his hangouts was the Benjamin Franklin Library, which housed a collection of English-language poetry. He recalls reading some of the American "establishment" poets whom he had studied in graduate school, like Robert

Lowell, Richard Wilbur, W.S. Merwin, and W.D. Snodgrass, though none excited him, as well as others whose poems he liked more, like Philip Booth and Ted Hughes. This was his first serious introduction to contemporary poetry, and he was intrigued.

Husband and wife returned to New York City in the late summer of 1965, and Charles began editorial work on a freelance basis in the reference department of a small publishing company whose chief editor was an acquaintance of Charles' Columbia advisor, John Unterecker. Although Charles was successful in editing—Unterecker reported his friend's calling Charles "the editing find of the century"—he found the work tedious and unrewarding. He had begun to write poems, partly under the influence of Theodore Roethke, and showed a few to Unterecker. Unterecker, himself a poet, suggested that he attend the New School poetry workshop being taught by his colleague Kenneth Koch. Charles, though, was timid and delayed a year, enrolling in the fall of 1966:

> I kept putting it off—probably out of sheer *insecurity*— but finally did enroll in Kenneth's poetry workshop, and it turned out to be the last time that he taught there.

The year of Koch's final New School workshop, 1966, was a sad time for the New York City poetry world because of the death of Frank O'Hara. To this day Charles regrets not having taken the workshop earlier, one reason being that he might have had a chance to meet the legendary O'Hara (who himself had taught a workshop there some years earlier). Luckily, the workshop with Koch was a profoundly important experience for Charles—a real turning point. He explains that "really, everything I did with respect to poetry at the beginning was a result of Kenneth's teaching." In particular, he enjoyed the excitement Kenneth brought to poetry and appreciated his assignments, which included writing poems in the style of American poets like William Carlos Williams and Walt Whitman. He soon published his first handful of poems in the mimeographed magazines connected to the newly established St. Mark's Poetry Project.

Charles stopped working freelance after the workshop as a result of being offered a teaching job in the English Department at Pace University in Manhattan. The job came about through meeting the poet Anne Waldman's mother, Frances, in Koch's workshop, and subsequently Anne; John Waldman, Anne's father, was an administrator at Pace and had been Chairman of the English Department.

Koch's workshop was eventually taken over by a young poet named Bill Berkson, and for a time Charles sat in on it, but after the initial inspiration from Koch, his poetry "floundered" for a couple of years, despite the efforts of Berkson, whom he came to know socially and admired. In hindsight, he understands his difficulty as the product of leaving "the beloved teacher" and having to find one's own way: "I don't think it's so strange in retrospect. It took me a while to figure out what I could do, what I wanted to do, and if I could really be a poet. It took a good two or three years before I started doing anything I liked again."

THE BREAKTHROUGH YEAR

> I am moved often, and easily
> without knowing why or finding it appropriate
> to be a consequence of somebody else's unfathomable will.
> —from "A Few Facts About Me" (1974)

Charles' self-proclaimed "breakthrough" came in the spring of 1970, when he sat in on a spring poetry workshop offered by Tony Towle at the Poetry Project. He was at a point where he had seriously considered giving up on poetry, so Tony's entrance into his life was a significant event. Tony encouraged Charles and to this day Charles credits Tony's enthusiasm, intelligence, and seriousness about poetry as a vocation with his own decision to stick to writing. He quickly fell into the habit of showing Tony just about everything he wrote and often received helpful handwritten feedback. In the tradition of his own mentor Frank O'Hara, Tony was generous with his time and was happy to drink with students after class at the nearby Orchidia Restaurant, where beer and pizza were served. Not knowing many people in the poetry world, Charles was excited by the opportunity to socialize with Tony and other young poets.

It was during the workshop that he met Paul Violi. Feeling less alone now that he had Tony and Paul as friends, Charles gradually began to meet the poets of his generation, many of whom considered the Poetry Project home base. At that time, Anne Waldman, who was four years Charles' junior and whose family home on McDougal Street was a sometime hangout for the Saint Mark's contingent, directed the Project. Charles fondly remembers the first party he attended at the Waldman townhouse, which he thinks occurred while he was taking Tony's workshop or shortly after its conclusion, and which was one of the first times he felt like a *real* poet.

> I met a bunch of poets who had been just names to me beforehand; they were eventually peers, but certainly not yet. I remember being tipsy and I particularly remember meeting Peter Schjeldahl and his asking me all sorts of questions, only some of which I was able to answer. What was most important was how excited I was to be in a big room filled with poets! That had never happened before. But I did feel like an outsider.... Although most of the poets were around my age, they were already part of a group and

I was just beginning. At least it helped me to feel that I wasn't the only poet, and that it was okay to be one!

The workshop also led to Charles' first poetry reading. Each workshop teacher selected one participant to give a reading at the Project. In spring 1970 Charles and a young poet named Rebecca Wright were chosen. As the evening of the reading approached, he experienced tremendous anxiety—so much so that before the reading he had several beers at a nearby bar, which ended up complicating his reading experience, to put it mildly. He believes that the alcohol kept him from connecting with either the poems or the audience, and he left feeling crestfallen.

Regardless of how he thought the reading went, he was beginning to be known as a poet, at least around the Poetry Project. But as most artists learn, being thought of as an artist by other artists does not guarantee that the genius committee will knock on your door. Charles was thirty, with no published book, and without the academic credentials needed to secure a tenure track job in English. In fact, during a budget crunch at Pace in 1971, he was let go as a full-timer and began instead to teach as an adjunct. Some of his poems from this general period reflect the uncertainty he was feeling, although they never enter into a transparently confessional mode of expression:

> Now that I am seeing myself as a totally different person
> whose interests are like a street covered with slush
> and whose every word rings like the ear of a spaniel
>
> night joins with its various egos, its tubeless containers
> of islands being joined by the notion of paradise
> and I am swept up in what it means to be drained...
>
> —from "Poem" (1974)

In addition to failing to live up to his parents' ideas about what he could become professionally, Charles continued to feel like an outsider around Saint Mark's. For starters, he didn't live on the Lower East Side; it took him 35–40 minutes to get to a reading. In addition, his life was more family-oriented than that of many of his poet acquaintances. Although he would meet other poets at readings and afterwards for drinks, he spent the majority of his non-working hours at home on the Upper West Side with Paula. Unlike many of his poet friends, he wasn't a heavy drinker; nor did he do drugs.

Although he continued to have difficulty thinking of himself as a poet—he rarely mentioned his work to strangers—he began to write and publish more than formerly, mostly in the cheaply produced Poetry Project magazine, *The World*, and satellite magazines such as *Telephone*, and *Adventures in Poetry* (which he felt was the best poetry magazine around), but also in the prestigious *Poetry* (Chicago), which accepted his poems the first time he submitted there. *Poetry* was perhaps the best-known poetry magazine in the country, and it was where many significant American poets, like John Ashbery, had received their first national publications. When he self-published ("hesitantly," he recalls) a chapbook of poems composed in the form of baseball lineups, accompanied by Paula's line drawings, in 1972, he mailed copies not only to poet friends and others but to his then favorite sportswriter, the *New York Post* columnist Larry Merchant, who to Charles' surprise phoned for an interview and then wrote two *Post* columns about *Lineups*, the second of which led to a large and favorable reader response.

He was invited by the sports historian Lee Lowenfish to speak about the book on WBAI radio, and remembers the writer Roger Angell as one of the other guests. He did a second set of "lineups" some fifteen years later—they have been reprinted in several anthologies and are now collected along with newer ones in *Complete Lineups* (2009). The lineups are among Charles' best-known poetic creations. Using the familiar American form of a baseball lineup, Charles metaphorically organizes a vast array of objects and human experiences— e.g., seasons, cities, vegetables, continental philosophers, diseases, Wordsworth poems—by batting order and field position. The disease lineup, for example, reads:

Polio rf

Syphilis (Gonorrhea) lf

Heart Disease ss

Cancer cf

Hepatitis 1b

Cirrhosis 3b

Measles c

Common Cold 2b

Influenza p

And the lineup dedicated to herbs and spices:

Mint 3b

Rosemary ss

Thyme lf

Salt 1b

Garlic c

Oregano rf

Dry Mustard cf

Vanilla 2b

Nutmeg p

The response to Charles' poetic idea, especially from readers who knew baseball, was very gratifying. In addition to being original and amusing, on a quasi-philosophical level the lineups organized objects, people, places, and ideas in a manner that illuminated unspoken and unexpected connections between things in the world. Although deceptively simple, the lineups succeeded in creating aesthetic playfulness while simultaneously exploring the associations and relations that helped order a chaotic universe.

ASSOCIATION WITH JAMES SCHUYLER

8/3

Dense fog during the night and early morning. Late
yesterday you could see it begin to flow and flatten
back against the cliff of the Berkshires, very white and
dreamlike…

—from "Aug.–Dec. For Jimmy Schuyler" (1999)

In the early '70s, Charles met his poetic hero James Schuyler, whose work he had been introduced to during Kenneth Koch's New School Workshop. In the spring of 1970, Charles showed Tony Towle a poem he had dedicated to Schuyler called "Lights"— it was published in his book *Elizabethan & Nova Scotian Music* (1974) —and Tony, who had known Schuyler for some years, sent it to him. A few months later, and very much out of the blue, a poem, "Light From Canada" (which Charles still thinks is one of Schuyler's very best), came in the mail with a dedication—*for Charles North*—and a gloss explaining an allusion to a line of O'Hara's, and a note saying, "Let me return the compliment." Charles was amazed and delighted. About a year later, again via Tony, Charles met Schuyler at a party in Morris Golde's apartment in the West Village. Golde was a businessman who was involved with contemporary music and the arts in general. Charles thinks, though he is not 100% certain, that this was the same party where he rubbed shoulders with Leonard Bernstein. He doesn't remember who actually introduced him to "Jimmy," but recalls being almost literally dumbfounded and very embarrassed about it afterward. "We just stood there standing across from one another, neither of us saying much."

Schuyler grew to admire Charles' work a great deal, and wrote a laudatory blurb for *Leap Year*, which reads, "His joy in words, and the things words adumbrate, is infectious: we catch a contagion of enlightenment. To me, he is the most stimulating poet of his generation." Charles recalls asking Jimmy if he really wanted to say that he was "the most stimulating poet of his generation" given that his generation included such poets as Towle, Ron Padgett, Ted Berrigan, Anne Waldman, Michael Brownstein, and others; Schuyler, however, was emphatic, both in his praise of Charles and when talking about him to others. In a letter to artist Trevor Winkfield dated March 31, 1971, Schuyler writes (speaking about a number of younger poets whose work he had recently gotten to know), "The one I most particularly liked was Charles North, who studied (at Saint Mark's Church, maybe?, or the New School) with Tony Towle. I think he has quite a gift." Charles didn't know about the extent of Schuyler's praise until Schuyler's letters were published by Turtle Point Press in 2004. He says, "It might have made a big difference to my confidence had I been aware how much he really thought of my poems back then."

To this day, Charles regrets not knowing Schuyler "when Jimmy was younger and healthier." Schuyler suffered from bouts of mental illness, which could result in disturbing breakdowns, one of which occurred while the poet Ron Padgett, his wife, and young son were staying with Schuyler one summer at the painter Fairfield Porter's home in Southampton, Long Island. After exhibiting unusual behavior, Schuyler descended the staircase with rose petals stuck to his naked body and demanded to know where Frank was (referring to Frank O'Hara, who had died several years earlier). Charles, luckily, never saw Schuyler at his worst:

> When he used to come over for dinner here in the late '70s he was often silent and looked unwholesome, to put it mildly. He would play steadily with his false teeth with his tongue—at least that's what it looked like. But he never acted crazy. Once after dinner—I don't know whether he was especially tired or didn't feel well, or what—he asked if he could sleep over. We were a little nervous about it, especially as Jill, my daughter, was very young at the time, but it was already late and of course we couldn't just turn him out. After a quiet night—for him anyway—he left in the morning. I do remember him requesting eggnog more than once when he was here for dinner in the winter, and my going downstairs in the snow to get him a quart, which he drank straight down.

Together, Charles and Jimmy edited two literary anthologies: *Broadway* (1979, with a cover by Paula) and then—a decade later—*Broadway 2* (cover by Trevor Winkfield). The first came about when Charles told Jimmy how much he admired a mimeo magazine that Schuyler had edited some years before, *49 South*. Charles still thinks of *Broadway* as "something between a mag and an anthology" of poems and drawings. He remembers some mild drama surrounding the editorial process: "We met to hash out the (sometimes thorny!) issue of contributors. He was plenty tough, and had no use for some of those I suggested—at least originally." Once they agreed upon a list of contributors, they invited everyone to "send us your best poem or drawing."

ELIZABETHAN & NOVA SCOTIAN MUSIC

What will see us through, a certain calm
Born of the willingness to be not cowed
The begonia idea of the universe
And because life is so short
A way of being unfaithful like the tide
Minus its characteristic awareness.

—from "Elizabethan & Nova Scotian Music" (1974)

About a year after the first *Lineups*, in the winter of 1973, Charles and Paula were invited to Lita and Morton Hornick's annual artists and poets party at their Park Avenue apartment. A patron of the arts, Lita Hornick also operated the Kulchur Foundation and Press. Charles recalls being excited by the invitation. Chatting with Larry Fagin, whom he barely knew other than as the editor and publisher of *Adventures in Poetry* magazine (which Charles had been published in) and chapbooks, Charles mentioned a manuscript he was putting together with the idea of self-publishing it as he had done previously with *Lineups*. To his delight, Fagin asked to see the manuscript, helped whittle it down editorially, and published it the following year as a chapbook with cover and drawings by Jane Freilicher (which also delighted Charles, as he loved her work, and in addition she was a close friend of, and collaborator with, the New York poets who had come to be his heroes). The book's title, *Elizabethan & Nova Scotian Music*, referred to the title of a record album of Elizabethan & Jacobean music he owned and to a trip to Nova Scotia he and Paula had recently taken. The trip partly grew out of Charles' great interest in the work of Elizabeth Bishop, who had written poetry about the Nova Scotian landscape and people in collections like *North & South* and *Questions of Travel*.

With Schuyler's encouragement, Charles mailed a copy to Bishop and received a letter in return:

Dear Mr. North:

Thank you for sending me ELIZABETHAN & NOVA SCOTIAN MUSIC (of course that title seems almost direct address [sic] to me!)—and I'm glad you like "Cape Breton," written so long ago now.... I'm sorry your book didn't come a week earlier, when I was having the "spring break" as Harvard calls it—now I'm sorry to say I am hard at work again and I haven't had time to do more than read through the poems very rapidly. I saw a great many things that I liked and that interested me very much. Please believe that as soon as I can, perhaps on a weekend, I'll really read them all over again and with attention and you'll be hearing from me again....

Charles says that if the "Elizabethan" in his title was a pun, it was an unconscious one. Bishop died several years later, and Charles was disappointed that she didn't in fact write again and that he never got to meet her. He was hearing positive things about his work from other sources, however. In a 1989 review of *Elizabethan & Nova Scotian Music*, the poet and art critic Barry Schwabsky reminisces about coming across the chapbook at the Gotham Book Mart on 47th St. in Manhattan:

A long time ago a book with a fine landscape drawing on the cover (by Jane Freilicher) caught my eye. I'd never heard of the poet, but somehow this promised something out of the ordinary. It was *Elizabethan & Nova Scotian Music*, Charles North's 1974 Adventures in Poetry mimeo.

I took the book home ($2.50 wasn't much of a risk even then) and near the beginning (in a poem called "To the Book") I read this:

> Open poetry died with Whitman.
> Closed poetry died with Yeats.
> Natural poetry was born and died with Lorca
> and Clare, also with France's Jean de Meun.

I was hooked. I knew this guy knew something I didn't—something none of the other poets I knew knew either. I also saw that this was something he somehow kept to himself, even as he offered it with open hands. So it was the true poetic mystery.

Although it was a limited printing and did not get much circulation outside New York, *Elizabethan & Nova Scotian Music* made an impression around the Poetry Project. Several years later Charles joined his close friend Paul Violi as co-publisher and -editor of Swollen Magpie Press, which Violi had begun earlier with the writer Allan Appel. North and Violi eventually published ten chapbooks, among them work by Joseph Ceravolo, Mary Ferrari, and Yuki Hartman, as well as Towle, Violi and North himself, in addition to *Broadway*. This collaboration, in addition to a chapbook he collaborated on with Tony called *Gemini*, cemented his relationship with his two good friends.

FATHERHOOD

Suppose I am not the uplifter of all I uplift,
   in the same sense that the coal-black sky, scumbled and
      showing a

few red streaks,

doesn't exactly equal space.

> —from "Day After Day The Storm Mounted.
> Then It Dismounted" (2001)

Paula and Charles had their first child, Jill, the same year that Larry Fagin published *Elizabethan & Nova Scotian Music*. A son, Michael, was born nine years later. Over the years that followed, Charles spent a good deal of time doing the things that fathers who are involved with their children do: changing diapers, taking the kids to school, attending the music and sports events they participated in, and seeing to it that they had as good an education as possible.

Charles did some writing when his children were small, but produced work that he was proud of only rarely. He characterizes himself even today as a fast writer but a slow finisher, who does "a lot of scribbling, not much keeping, and a fair amount of putting away and later—sometimes much later—relocating (in both senses)." Slowly but surely, though, the books came out. In 1977, he published the chapbook *Six Buildings*, followed by *Leap Year* (1978), *The Year of the Olive Oil* (1989), *No Other Way* (selected prose mostly about artists, critics, and poets, 1998), *New and Selected Poems* (1999), *The Nearness of the Way You Look Tonight* (2001), *Cadenza* (2007), *Complete Lineups* (2009), *Ode to Asparagus, Peonies and Manet* (chapbook essay, 2010), *What It Is Like: New and Selected Poems* (2011), and *Translation* (2014). His work was selected for inclusion in Scribner's *Best American Poetry* Series in 1995 and 2002, as well as in a number of other important anthologies. And in the late '90s, his sometimes tenuous position in the Pace University English Department was reconfigured with Pace naming him its first full-time Poet-in-Residence.

CHARLES NORTH

Helping to raise a family was a central part of Charles' life from Jill's birth in 1974 until Mike's departure for college in 2002. Whereas some artists and poets see family as a distraction from their work, Charles looks back upon the infancy, childhood, and teenage years of Jill and Michael with immense feeling and pride and no small degree of nostalgia.

Charles' mother died of complications from emphysema during the winter of 1980. Shortly after her death, his father began exhibiting the first signs of Alzheimer's disease, from which he died eight years later. Following his wife's death, he had remarried and moved to Florida. His father's illness was "overwhelming" and "difficult to see past," particularly as Charles had to take over most of his father's affairs. Ironically, Schuyler approached Charles around this time and asked if he would be his co-literary executor along with the painter Darragh Park, a request that he had to turn down due to the practical and emotional burden his father's condition imposed on him. It was especially hard coming to terms with making decisions for his father, a man who had seemed, even in Charles' adult life, not only capable but formidable. Some years ago Charles found a grotesque photograph of his father taken in his Florida nursing home after he had become virtually insensible to his surroundings; after some agonizing, Charles tore up the photo.

LITERARY RECOGNITION

Aug. 4. I am in front of a larger college audience about to give my opening Charles Eliot North Lecture, but before I can utter a word someone asks a question and I spend the entire time trying to answer it....

—from "Summer Of Living Dangerously" (2007)

When I asked about his career as a poet, Charles responded that only in the late '90s did it appear to gain some momentum. Several fortuitous events took place. In 2001 he was awarded his second NEA Creative Writing Fellowship; John Ashbery chose his book *The Nearness of the Way You Look Tonight* as one of five finalists for the inaugural Phi Beta Kappa Poetry Award for best poetry book of the year; and he gave a reading with Ashbery at the Sackler Auditorium at Harvard University. Although he had known John casually for years, this was the first occasion that he had actually spent time with him. Prior to this he had been shy in his presence.

The reading, introduced by Jorie Graham (Charles recalls Helen Vendler in the audience), turned out to be a great success, as a result of which a few hundred Harvard and M.I.T. undergraduates, graduate students, professors, and community members came to know North's work for the first time. The *Harvard Crimson* interviewed North and Larry Fagin, Adventures in Poetry's co-editor (the reading was arranged because books by Charles and John Ashbery had kicked off the newly revived press), and did a big piece on the two poets.

A handful of honors have come Charles' way over the last decade, although, as John Jacob pointed out in *The American Book Review* (2000) apropos Charles' original *New and Selected Poems*: "Many poets respect what North is doing, but the big prizes and fellowships have avoided him, and reading this book one can see why. This is not the material of the American Poetry Series. These poems would sooner be the fragments of the poems in those types of books. Sometimes the fragment should be the poem, and we need poets like Charles North to remind us of that."

In 2005 he was awarded his fourth Fund For Poetry Award, and in 2008 he received a substantial Individual Artist's Grant from the Foundation for Contemporary Arts. *What It Is Like: New and*

Selected Poems was chosen by the *New York Times* critic David Orr to head NPR's list of Best American Poetry Books of 2011.

Apropos the Phi Beta Kappa Award, one experience affected him deeply. He and the other four finalists—Kenneth Koch, Ann Lauterbach, Amy Gerstler, and Dara Wier—gave a group reading at the Library of Congress, hosted by Billy Collins, then U.S. Poet Laureate. For Charles, as exciting as it was, the event was bittersweet because the winner, his former teacher Kenneth Koch, was in the advanced stages of leukemia, and although he gave what Charles describes as a heroic reading, it was obvious that he was dying. In fact, it would be his last large public reading before his death in July 2002. Charles remembers watching Kenneth walk slowly down the aisle of the Amtrak train they took down to Washington, D.C.:

> He didn't look like himself. His clothes hung on him. He had lost so much weight because of whatever was going on... the chemo. I knew he was very sick and I was actually surprised that he was making the trip. I think he knew, although I don't think it was officially announced, that he was going to get the award. We weren't told until we got down there.

When asked if he spent time with Kenneth during his final weeks, Charles responded:

> I couldn't bring myself to go to the hospital. I think Paul [Violi] might have gone, and I know David Shapiro spent a lot of time there. Again, I never knew Kenneth that well, and never felt really comfortable in his presence, any more than I did with Schuyler or Ashbery. That's the trouble, at least for me, with heroes, and father figures.

REGRETS AND ONGOING STRUGGLES

A laugher, as they say about certain baseball games.
Hollow-eyed (and in every other conceivable way).

—"Death's Victory" (from "Pictures from Bruegel," 2011)

At the end of our penultimate conversation I inquired if Charles had any pressing regrets about "the road(s) not taken" (e.g., whether he regretted not getting his Ph.D. or completing law school). We had been talking for nearly two hours at that point and the sunlight was beginning to slant across the living room wall. The answer was a flat "No!" He thinks he made the right occupational choices, partly by what seemed at the time like an accident, though he confesses to occasional regrets as a result of spending so many years in "the poetic shadows."

His omission from several anthologies—particularly after Carcanet Press in England had included him as one of the eleven poets in *New York Poets II* (the first volume consisted of Ashbery, Koch, O'Hara and Schuyler)—continues to rankle, though he understands the literary and social politics involved in anthology-making. Also, he remains more than a little frustrated by what he described in a 1991 lecture ("The State of the Art," printed in *American Poetry Review* the following year and reprinted in *No Other Way*) as the poetry world's "false reputations" (he thinks he picked up this phrase from Kenneth Koch), which are recognitions based on factors having little to do with the merit of work. He touched on this theme in a lengthy letter he wrote but wound up not sending (printed in *No Other Way*) to the *New York Review of Books* apropos an article on Schuyler by the noted Harvard University critic Helen Vendler:

[It was] as though she was attending to him [Schuyler] not because she really liked or truly admired the poetry, but because he had won a prize, had been nominated for another, and in addition had published a book-length poem. In that sort of climate of readers and critics, it's hard to imagine poets getting their due for the right reasons if at all....

Regret aside, Charles acknowledges that life has been good to him. He has been happily married to a woman whom he loves and deeply admires, as he also admires and loves his two successful, well-adjusted children. He finds it exciting that his daughter and her husband are both successful philosophers, one of the careers he chose not to pursue.

When I asked what the hardest part of being a father has been, Charles paused reflectively—stating at first that "It's a hard question to answer; I mean I've enjoyed so much about it. I do remember how tough it was to watch my quarterback son getting slammed to the ground! Or sleeping sometimes on the floor of his room when he was five and wheezing from spring asthma. Or Paula and me lying awake anxiously at 3:00 or 4:00 a.m. waiting for Jill (who had *left* the house at midnight) to come back from a date or friends—or at least call to let us know she was still alive!" Jill, now in her late thirties, is a philosopher of physics at Cornell University, and Mike, who recently received his Ph.D. in Social Psychology from Princeton, specializes in ageism and is currently a Post-Doctoral Fellow at Columbia. Both are married and Jill and her husband Ted have two daughters of their own. Whenever Charles talks about his children he has a warm twinkle in his eye. He delights in their accomplishments, as well as in how they've turned out as people. Although he is not one to boast, he is clearly happy to report how well their lives seem to be going. Still, he and Paula miss seeing their children as often as they once did:

Mike's very, very busy; Jill's very, very busy, as well as out of town. We sometimes have to make appointments for telephone calls! Of course Jill has been on her own for a quite a while now, but until a couple of years ago, she was around, living in the city and commuting to teach at Yale. I love them both so much that it's been hard to adjust. I do have to add that both are wonderful about visiting. Ithaca hasn't stopped Jill, nor, when Mike lived in Jersey City, did the P.A.T.H. train stop him—and we do travel to them when we can.

Charles is in good health, despite an aortic valve replacement in 2001 (which had to be redone about nine years later), right about the time of his sixtieth birthday. Looking back upon the initial surgery, he reports having been unprepared for the crushing post-operative depression that came over him:

> There is an intriguing theory that the depression has something to do with the fact that you've been on a heart and lung machine so your heart has been literally out of your body—there is an invasion of the self in this complex way that nobody fully understands. I really don't know. I wasn't prepared for it because the surgeon didn't talk about it, nobody did! Only afterwards did I meet a couple of people who had had similar experiences.

A private person, Charles talked about his depressed state mostly to Paula. When I pressed him a bit, asking whether he wishes he had friends he could share his more private thoughts and feelings with, he went on to say: "I'm not that kind of person, so it doesn't bother me. We have these kinds of boundaries."

During that difficult summer, Charles was unable to do much writing, but did make some notes—some of which had to do with Koch's diagnosis of aggressive leukemia—that were the raw material for a long poem, "Summer of Living Dangerously." He made more notes for "Summer of Living Dangerously" the next summer, when Koch in fact died. He feels that Koch's illness along with his own surgery underlie the lengthy poem, which is mostly in prose, in the form of a diary that chronicles forty-five days (or clusters of days) in 2001 from June 16th until September 30th.

Recent years have been full and positive—with the exception of an unexpected and very difficult event: the death of his close friend and fellow poet Paul Violi in the spring of 2011. He continues to dream about Paul. In losing his friend, Charles also lost the poet to whom, for more than two decades, he had showed just about every poem he wrote before showing it to anyone else—as Violi did to him. Paula had done the cover for Violi's first big book, *In Baltic Circles* (1973), as well as drawings for *Harmatan* (1977), and the Norths and Violis had been friends since the '70s. As for Charles' second surgery, though he had to leave his classes in the middle of the fall term, he was able to return in the spring, and he feels that, all in all, he was able to handle both the surgery and recuperation better than the first time around. Following recuperation, he was as active as he was before, exercising and walking a lot, and playing golf occasionally—and "occasionally well"—with an old clarinetist friend.

And there have been happy goings-on to do with family and poetry. Jill has published important articles in her specialty, the philosophy of physics, and Mike has begun to publish on the topic of ageism in respected psychology journals. In 2011 Jill's husband, Theodore Sider, a prominent philosopher in metaphysics and logic, published *Writing the Book of the World* to widespread acclaim. In the summer of 2011 Mike married Meghan Lewis, whom he had begun dating at the University of Michigan, and in late November of that year, Charles' big new and selected poems, *What It is Like*, was published. And the Norths became grandparents: Polly was born to Jill and Ted in December 2010, with Jane to follow almost exactly two years later. Meanwhile, Charles has continued to teach honors and poetry courses at Pace as well as run a Poets @ Pace series that has featured readings by noted poets.

THE FUTURE

I like very much the notion that I will
Appear in another life…

         —from "Madrigal: Another Life" (1974)

"What is it that you still want to accomplish?" I asked him recently, a question that he was reluctant to answer. He did say that he would like to continue to write poems he is "proud of" and eventually to collect them in a new book, as well as to publish an expanded edition of his literary and art essays. When I asked about whether he would like to retire from teaching, he stated that he cannot do so for economic reasons, although he would like eventually to teach, say, one class per semester as a transition into retirement. For now, he still enjoys teaching both young poets and literature classes, and he gets a special kick out of his involvement in the Pace Honors program, where he has had the chance to construct his own courses, including one he titled "The Pleasures of Poetry." He looks forward to watching his granddaughters grow up. He would love to break 85 on the golf course despite his infrequent play and the increasing unlikelihood he will do so. When I broach the subject of death and dying, Charles stops me.

WORK

Charles North cares a great deal about line breaks, word choices, and how a poem looks on the page, though he hopes the behind-the-scenes work isn't obvious to readers. He recalls with some gratification submitting "A Note on Labor Day," a poem that took a long time to get "right," years ago to an anthology being edited by Howard Moss, then poetry editor of *The New Yorker*, and Moss congratulating him on the poem's "spontaneity." Although he believes he's getting "looser," he still finds occasionally that getting a poem right can entail a multiyear or even a decade-long process. As he put it in a 2001 *Poetry Project Newsletter* interview with Ange Mlinko, "I don't write slowly, but I *finish* slowly. Too slowly. I don't labor over poems, but I'm always putting things into a drawer and then not liking them enough when I pull them out again. At my worst, it can take years of putting in and taking out! ... I do scribble in notebooks, but only a small portion of the scribbling amounts to anything. As you can see, I don't believe in Ginsberg's 'First Thought. Best Thought' [laughs]."

Charles seems more than a little interested in the poetics of form; and the majority of his poems have internal logics that emerge from unique sets of aesthetic parameters and rules. Take the lineups, for example. His love and extensive knowledge of baseball, which date back to childhood, yielded a deeply personal calculus for determining relationships between various field positions and batting orders. The first lineup in his 1972 chapbook goes:

> San Francisco   ss
> Munich   cf
> Paris   lf
> Rome   c

```
Madrid      3b
London      rf
Athens      1b
Istanbul    2b
New York    p
```

The implications of these cities and their positions on the baseball field could take many spirited hours of conversation to explore. Is Charles offering a poetic commentary on the geopolitics of 1972, or does the lineup reflect a subjectively cryptic relationship to these places based upon the triumphs, disappointments, fantasies, and regrets of his own life? Not to mention the fact that the reader may cluster his or her own complicated web of personal, historical/cultural, and political associations around the place names. The form of the poem unleashes a world of imaginative possibilities.

A quick glance through *What It Is Like* reveals a surprising number of forms from villanelles and triolets to invented schemes. Charles has written in rare and under-utilized forms (e.g., the Japanese haibun), added something fresh to familiar poetic forms like the pantoum, and played off and/or parodied traditional form, as in his fragmentary rhyming couplets "Fourteen Poems." The long poem "Building Sixteens" has a form entirely of his own making. Here's how he explained it in an email to me:

> You're welcome to know what I know about it... sixteen 16-line stanzas (the title and original idea are from the card game Casino, which I played endlessly as a child). I thought of them as sonnet-like, and the extra impetus (the "building") was to have each section come to an apparent conclusion but then turn out to continue in the next. Someone once said to

me that with the indented lines they had the look of "building blocks," but if so, that was unconscious on my part.

The final "building" reads:

[16]

and let's hope, given the nature of light
and *its* celestial ambitions that the
time doesn't simply erode, but offers
shoppers the chance to pile into their
      wagons and the row houses
      ahead, evicting above all
      the object-less now that
      some of the foolish ideas have
      been doffed for what they
      are, assemblages whose
      flickerings of life and color
      preclude the ship and its margins.
Forkfuls in shady plots, toward acreage
above all the bars and reflected sunsets,
the chief cup for mailmen here on earth,
      decanters filled with wine and express civic virtue.

The carefully constructed quality of the "buildings" contours a rich and varied linguistic landscape that lacks an ounce of superfluous fat. There is no filler in Charles' poems. Another thing that one doesn't find much of in Charles' work is autobiographical confession. Readers hoping to encounter Charles on a Mary Oliver-esque amble through a meadow at daybreak, or embarking upon the clever shenanigans and reflections that populate the work of Billy Collins, may feel let down. Aside from the possible exceptions of "A Note on Labor Day" and "The Summer of Living Dangerously," few of his poems are autobiographical—at least not in an explicitly self-revelatory manner. The following fragments typify the closest that Charles gets to personal confession. "A Note on Labor Day," which took nearly a decade to complete and is dedicated to his wife, is personal:

> And I seem to be
> lost again, if that doesn't
> sound too dramatic,
> and this time seems worse,
> or around the slightly silvered bend
> slightly blurred in late sun
> that has some whirling filters over it
> mostly for the jackets and the books.

And in "Summer of Living Dangerously," tumultuous emotions are expressed as threatening weather patterns. As mentioned earlier, the poem was written over two of the most emotionally difficult summers of Charles' life—a period marked by recovery from open-heart surgery—and then, one summer later, the death of Kenneth Koch:

> Aug. 6. A pretty good morning: clear, well-defined clouds;
> no over-reaching. Towards mid-day less well-defined so the
> reach was ambiguous—ultimately prophetic as it darkened
> uncontrollably and began to pour and never stopped. So:
> an alert start, followed by a short but emblematic gray
> area, and a largely bitter, peaty finish.

The non-confessional nature of Charles' work is in part explained by the reserved type of person that he is, in addition to his aesthetic preference for how a poem *works* over what a poem is *about*. A rather poetic-looking list he designed for the initial meeting of an honors literature class he created at Pace University illustrates this preference. An emphasis on function is apparent in the two contrasting lists—both of which present pleasure-producing poetic attributes. The lists suggest that aesthetic pleasure can be produced in an infinite number of ways.

LIT 211 D: A Very Partial List of Some Pleasures of Poetry (with overlappings)

Pleasures Of	Pleasures Of
Flow, melody, cohesion	Disruption, dissonance, dislocation, parataxis
Clarity	Mystery, confusion, suggestion, evocation
Form	Formlessness, invented forms
Feeling, emotion	Story-telling, description, intellect, imagination
Logic, reason	Association, illogic, "craziness"
Seriousness	Humor, parody, wit
Adulthood	Childishness, silliness
The private (secret)	The public
Quietness, modesty	Loudness, egocentricity
Familiarity, expectation, tradition	Originality, surprise
Depth, profundity	Surface, superficiality, jotting
Easiness	Difficulty, challenge, provocation
Good taste	Bad taste, outrageousness
Brevity	Length, "ongoingness"
"Subjects," making sense	Word-play, music of the language
Rule-following	Rule-breaking

Truth	Fiction, lying
Verse	Poetry written in prose
Beauty	Realism, difficult experience, unpleasantness
Elegance	Awkwardness, jarring, colloquialism
Satisfaction, conclusion	Just stopping, being left "up in the air"
Reading poetry	Hearing poems read, writing poems
Good poetry	Bad poetry

When I asked him what it was that he imagined readers of his work get (after all, only a minority of poetry readers think about function), Charles made reference to this course and its premise that poems can offer a great variety of pleasures on many levels. "I like to surprise myself in the hope that I will surprise readers, among other things by making poetry out of unlikely materials." For instance, the final entry from "Summer of Living Dangerously" considers the notion of a rigid designator, first introduced by the analytic philosopher Saul Kripke in his groundbreaking work *Naming and Necessity* (1980). A rigid designator, according to Kripke, "designates" the same thing in all possible worlds in which that thing exists, and does not designate anything else in those possible worlds in which that thing doesn't exist. Charles subjects this notion to a range of reflections, writing for example that "the use of a rigid designator for something or someone who no longer exists brings with it a poignancy that can sometimes verge on the intolerable." The final sentence of the thirteen-page poem coalesces the entries into a stunning meditation on impermanence and loss:

And yet we continue to use it (or pretend to use it) in the same way, even though the reference itself is cut off almost before it has a chance to get started, so that it is really more of a stammer than a reference, a stammered reference, the non-referential aspect becoming clearer as well as increasingly poignant as time passes.

One suddenly finds oneself looking at the technical concept of a rigid designator in an emotional way, which isn't exactly a common response to analytic philosophy, but that's just fine because this is a poem after all. Along these lines, Charles hopes that his use of "unlikely materials" might stimulate, surprise, move or amuse readers, bringing pleasure in some of the same ways a painting or sonata might—and not merely at superficial levels, but deeply.

In addition to the element of surprise, the musical cadences of Charles' language produce pleasure. As suggested above, he has a reputation for making lyrical poems out of material that is anything but lyrical, elevating mundane and technical-sounding verbiage into poetry. His effervescent lines can have the music you hear when reading the poetry of Wordsworth or Keats. This comes across when one reads a North poem silently, and then a second time aloud. The music helps to carry readers through language that is often heady and abstract, even at times nearing the inaccessible. But despite its difficulty and absence of specific personal reference, Charles' work is palpably personal. Beneath its meticulously polished surfaces, one feels the muted rise and fall of emotional waves.

Charles feels that his recent work is more open than his earlier work, freer emotionally, and less muted. "I think my poems these days are messier than they used to be," he wrote shortly after the publication of *Cadenza* in 2007, "which I hope is a good thing, some sort of departure. The long poems that begin and end the new book, *Cadenza*, are, in this sense, more cadenza-like...." A "cadenza" is a musical term that refers to a section of a concerto when an orchestra stops, leaving a soloist to play in free time, alone. When the cadenza ends, the orchestra usually re-enters and finishes the movement on its own. A significant part of this freedom involves being more open, which, in addition to making his work more "cadenza-like," led to a willingness to talk about himself. As he put it during one of our interviews, "Emotionally, I was pretty much bottled up for years. I wasn't very verbal.... I mean outwardly. Probably if you had known me twenty years ago you would have found me still fairly withdrawn. And now [echoing Frank O'Hara's poem "Autobiographia Literaria"] here I am at the center of language. Imagine!"

One characteristic of this openness, or freedom, is the frequent transformations that move through his stanzas like weather patterns: the non-lyrical into the lyrical; gloominess into humor; idea into idea in a steady stream that is as much conscious as it is unconscious. The stream encompasses a wide range of emotions, moods, tones, and themes. His poems contain frequent moments of joy, much of which is expressed in the form of verbal excitement and play—such as found in the opening three couplets of "Chain" (2000), which happens to be an example of end-to-beginning or "chain" rhyme, which he attempted because the challenge seemed "impossible":

> Russia is the domed incantation of Kansas
> As oceans burn in the individual day.
>
> All day they came and went, sheep dog
> Dogged social climber, sedulous

Luster after the Maison d'Infinite

In fine (it looks like) print, the curse of snowflakes.

These lines may reflect what James Schuyler meant when he wrote that "(Charles') *joy* [my ital.] in words, and the things words adumbrate, is infectious: we catch a contagion of enlightenment." The idea of Russia as "the domed incantation of Kansas" is as strange and original as the image of oceans burning "in the individual day." And the images of a sheep dog followed by a "dogged social climber," or snowflakes as a "curse," are as funny as they are unexpected. Although critics may find themselves stymied when it comes to analyzing these lines, the exuberance they convey needs little explication. They aren't describing a state of being (e.g., joy), *they are that state.*

The experience of hearing Charles read his work almost always educes a fair amount of laughter from an audience. In addition to humorous images, it's entertaining to watch Charles fight back his own laughter. The work contains moments of laugh-out-loud hilarity, such as when he asks the question, "Does the name R. Penis Blavatsky mean anything, at all, to you?" in "Day After Day the Storm Mounted. Then It Dismounted" (2000). The title was inspired by a voice-over in a Woody Woodpecker TV feature. But ebullience and humor seldom last before becoming something else. Charles is a composer of emotional and imagistic flux. The stimuli of New York City are perhaps nowhere more apparent than in the changes that push one part of a poem into another. Several pages into "Day After Day…" there's a melancholic shift punctuated by a strange, surrealistic image. Together the emotional swerve communicates the following sequence: life is exciting; no wait—life is exceedingly sad; no wait—the strangeness of life continually overwhelms us….

In fact, for a long time
I've felt like apologizing
for what seem to me excessive references to darkness
as though the available light were on trial.
Sometimes it's virtually impossible
to get up in the morning. The days in
the middle of winter when it doesn't begin
to get light till 7 a.m. or even later,
the swirl commandeering hydrants, curbstones,
stoops, etc. To brush back the shadows
from the cheek of night. "To be,"
as Thomas Browne wrote, "a kind of nothing
for a moment," a balloon with a beard…

Charles' lengthy "Summer of Living Dangerously," written while "death was in the air," contains a fair share of melancholy, as do a number of other poems in *Cadenza*. He was surprised when a New York poet and publisher he knows well told him that reading the poem from start to finish was like sitting through a stand-up comedy routine; from Charles' perspective, much of the poem is dark, haunted by the idea of dying. The poem's gravity is lightened, however, by comical and absurdist interludes. Two entries from the poem demonstrate this point:

Aug. 24. A long line of vehicles, from 18-wheelers to mountain bikes and those silver scooters that were so popular a couple of years ago, stacked up in front of a rural railroad crossing, ridge of foothills in the distance. Two large heavyset men in dark business suits and white socks, pants a little too short, lying on their sides on the grass intent on fixing something at track level.

The postcard version of life gets an unnecessarily bad rap. It's one among many, not necessarily false or reductive. To say it distorts the *tone* of life is to describe in a realistic manner an aspect of life that is as real as any other.

Aug. 25. Rain promised again—strange sort of promise— but zilch so far (mid-afternoon). Whole blocks of sky moving slowly as if painfully, or as if hiding something that would be painful if revealed.

Just before dusk a strip of bluish acetate like the thin wash of clouds the saints go marching in.

The moral of the story is that there is no single emotional tone that pervades a given poem; instead, emotion gives way to emotion in a manner that contrasts with the "bottled up" emotional life that Charles associates with his younger self—that is, who he was until he married Paula and until his life, with the help of poetry, began to pick up.

It was later on through poetry, as an adult, that he resumed what might be considered the musical part of his life that had been on hold. His attraction to form, pacing, and tone suggest the pervasive influence of his musical origins. Some of his earliest memories, once again, are of listening to his mother play the piano, and his early successes on the clarinet provided him with a sense of purpose and self-identity. It's no coincidence that the beautiful painting on the cover of *Cadenza* happens to be of an open clarinet case revealing the multiple pieces of his two instruments. The perspective of the painting, by Paula North, seems to invite the reader to reach down, assemble the clarinets, and play.

But old habits are hard to shake. During one of our interviews, Charles reported never being able to acknowledge fully the praise others offered him and that his teenage performances in all-county and all-state concert bands, and in orchestras and ensembles during his summers at Interlochen—as well as his solo performances— were almost always accompanied by anxiety. A similar anxiety has accompanied his poetic pursuits. To this day he occasionally introduces himself to others as a college teacher or writer rather than a poet—despite having published twelve collections of poetry over thirty years as well as a collection of prose pieces; having co-edited the anthologies *Broadway* and *Broadway 2* with James Schuyler; having won awards for his work; and having been given the title Poet-in-Residence at Pace University in Manhattan.

Why is this? One possible answer is the extent to which a proper vocation (e.g., becoming a lawyer or physician) was emphasized at least tacitly in Charles' upwardly mobile, Jewish household. Being a musician or poet never measured up to the ideas of success promoted by his parents. This hypothesis also helps to explain why the approval of Kenneth Koch, James Schuyler, and John Ashbery was so important to him. In addition to trying to launch his career, Charles entertains the possibility that he was seeking the endorsement of a father figure.

These factors help shed light on why he jumped from one profession to another as a young man. He was smart enough to excel at any profession he chose, but also smart enough to know at some level that he wouldn't be satisfied with a job that circumscribed his imagination. Although he could have had financially and socially rewarding careers in academic philosophy, law, literature or editing, he *chose* to become a poet—though he might say that poetry "chose" him. Instead of writing legal briefs or academic papers or editing reference books, he invested his imaginative life in the construction of poetic artifacts, the perimeters and rules of which were partly determined by "a tone or kind of language, or even a vague shape or length"—which he says he often has a sense of, prior to beginning a poem.

The work of Charles North is an important tributary of American poetry, and specifically New York School poetry, because it expands the possibilities of what a poem can be, while simultaneously falling within the continuum of the American lyrical tradition. In Charles' poetry one will encounter the quiet winter gazes of an Emily Dickinson, the ordering intellect of a Wallace Stevens, and the language games of a Gertrude Stein coalesced into the light touch of a classical musician who flirted with the idea of becoming a philosopher of aesthetics—but decided to dedicate his life to creating an aesthetics of his own. Stein wrote that to compose in words is to compose a way of being in the world. What Charles has created over his long career has both challenged and expanded traditional notions of what poetry is and how it can be experienced—in addition to placing a "clarinet" back into his hands. And it's with this figurative clarinet that Charles North has expressed himself in music beyond the meaning of words.

TONY TOWLE

Prologue

Only one at a time of mourning,
in which the edge of the hill
is going down
and I was close to loving you for it.

So this is a tale, then; good.
The forest is important,
the boar hunt,
and the close of the legend,

when by turns the leaves would arrive
with the next nice October
and the king was away from our throats.

Good. But not only that; later,
when the edge was folding
and we were not discussed,
more at the disposal
of Madame de Sévigné,

on the way to exorcism,
on the platform;
I might have wished that you were not the subject,
maimed and partly displayed.

The pilgrims are cautious and exact
and only a trickle comes to the edge.
I stir slightly.

TONY TOWLE

The residue, white, is hung
without sound.

The Hotel

The two knights suggest to the king that he take the hero
into his confidence. The pantomimes are spaced to accommodate
    them.
It is a work of great beauty. It is night. Four boys
remain on the scene. They choose four girls. This is what happens:
Her beauty and her brains work like fire. She is shocked
by his remark that he cannot spend too much time. We see grace of
body and mind being torn to pieces. Now begins the bitter
    aftermath.
Now the prayers of Orpheus are answered. It is the ancient
myth of Orpheus. Orpheus cannot console himself with his own
    song.
The song of the lyre is inadequate to his bereavement. Now he
    finishes
the song. Everything is green. Everything is splashed with color.

Nearing Christmas

A frog croaks continually in the pond below,
and jumps out onto the ground.
I climb through a window and cross the floor
past a forest of utensils.
A heard of bison roams the great plains;
they bite my hands so I feed them;
a girl paints a yellow sun streaked with orange,
the last of some lines before the Christmas rush,
before the wingless exasperations of Bloomingdale's
which already entwine my heels
in intellectual pursuit.
I knew it would happen eventually,
Frank's poems would come out
and I would feel the impulse to close up shop,
so I have sat down to write,
evading the personality, like Rimbaud,
jumping into one, like Marianne Moore,
or sitting simply like a sack of raisins in space
as you threaten to become my personal Rachmaninoff.

I have never been able to drink in the morning,
as opposed to Frank, to whom the day was of a piece,
the sun poised firmly in the middle of the sky,
though many a fortress has been lost in the meantime
and a snowy range of mountains rises behind them,
with some of the people forgotten,
cancelled out by pretty events.
I didn't meet Frank O'Hara in 1959, as in the book's notes,

we met in 1962, August, by chance in the Cedar Bar. In 1959
I hadn't even begun to write, and by 1962
the problem was neatly reversed,
having wept with love and irritation
beneath the honorable sky,
which leads everywhere at once.

December 15th, noon, 1971,
one quick drink and I'm off to Bloomingdale's,
crawling with ants on a Popsicle of moving clouds,
against the color of the junior sky, by extension
to Irma's coat, the far promontory, and the uniform of the person
who turns the handle
in Rachel's Musical Mystery House, the end of Part I
the road and the morning.

I'm still here, 12:22, perhaps three minutes fast,
forgetting what I was going to say.
Two more drinks Towle and you'll say anything.
I haven't been called Towle since high school.
I had something else to say but I don't remember what it was.
Two Spanish painters are painting my front door a tasteless orange,
one more anonymous tribute to "Why I Am Not a Painter."
Dr. Zhivago is a great novel, I don't care what anyone says.
I could have written *Safe Conduct* myself; in 1964
it occurred to me I might write one for Frank some day
if he ever died before I did, which wasn't likely.

TONY TOWLE

Well he did and I haven't.

Irma needs skirts

so I'm going to Bloomingdale's to look for some,

empty ones that is. I remember when it could be said

that someone had a dirty mind,

no more hopeless and antiquated than having, say,

the mind of Henry James.

"The woman's place is in the novel." —Henry James,

who would be sipping something more exotic;

but I have really got to go,

out through the door

to the facts of life.

My life at any rate is more oblique than Frank's.

What have I ever said to the sun, for example?

What did I ever say to Frank, for that matter,

brooding on the promontory of my early poetic development,

silent and self-preoccupied, garrulous and self-preoccupied,

not that anything's changed too much,

an aging Frank O'Hara Award winner

jumping from ice floe to ice floe,

a step ahead of a horde of younger practitioners,

to whom I nevertheless occasionally turn and shout some advice:

which is not to have a mistaken notion of your biography;

no event in your life is of the slightest importance,

but there is nothing you cannot use;

the unceasing events of your boring life

occur only for the success of a particular poem

awaiting your efforts on a horizon.

For instance, it is supposed that I am drunk at a party;
I walk unsteadily into the foyer
where Joe, Jane, and John are putting on their coats.
I stand there for a moment, breaking the alliteration,
then find my way back, staggering with the implications,
to the hors d'oeuvre of the infinite room
which I have chosen from the swirling elements,

from the actual events, stories, and people.
I don't see clearly the swirling elements,
I am made up of those elements;
it would be better to live *over* a dyke bar than *under* one;
like poetry they perhaps at worst only confuse two specialties,
itself with life in poetry's case.

Finally I have gone to Bloomingdale's
and I am back.
You call that lyric you big bag of shit?
I am not talking to myself,
or in that manner to a great poet of the past,
that must be Frank, talking to me;
I am at last fully awake in this mortal life,
for the few years in the middle,
and I keep myself opaque and I don't regret it,
on the promontory.

Frank you've got to help me

and there is an answer but not at this moment.

Autobiography

Prologue

With an eye for the ladies,
you lift up a skirt,
in New York,
in a brief reference to infinity,
and find a New York woman,
aghast at your manners
and amused by your lament.

I get up from the floor
my dear ladies (*donne mie care*),
a continuous line from the porch to the hammock,
and will tell you everything.
I close the door
and the doorknob hangs in space
on the other side.

For ten years I have courted the muse
through memories and despair, poverty,
the specters of urban development,
and the blood of an unbelievable impatience.

At a certain point my imagination began to stir, like boats,
sitting on a still horizon, moved by a gathering breeze,
torn apart in a tempest,
and by the nerves in the following calm.

At first I boiled the language, like an egg,
the spirit broken at the insufferable hands of sociology,
until at last the ground trembled and broke, like an egg,
and I could imagine filling some small need of literature's
as well as finally, and in a modest way, my own —
a stew of undergrowth and towering oaks.
From Europe my ancestors headed west, to a certain point,
then returned to the east in the logical irony of opposites,
to get lost on nature's accordion walls,
resolved in nature's immortal subterfuge

Yet I hesitate to give myself dramatic location,
time without place is my usual location,
someone from the last century thinking to be in the preceding one,
but without really mentioning anything specific
that happened in those centuries.
I return to my century and open up Spenser, and the sun,
an elevated plum and a demon from the dim past,
closes an eye on the ocean at sunset,
dropping from a plate to the carpet of green forest,
crushing the fragrant spices soaked by torrential rains,
echoes to my clinical romanticism
expressed with wit and a carrot boundary;
unhappiness, a curve in the river, a bight,
lemon sharks in the rainbow sunset,
a cataract of billiard residents
rolling from their intellectual core.

An eagle lands, for example, on vacation in the approaching dusk,
in a simple dénouement, a right to the solar plexus,

delivered like death in the Middle Ages,
free of rancor and sentimentality;
and a final dénouement,
a left to the jaw in the soft haze of dusk
where people even older than I
can still do marvelous things.
Of course our bodies are no longer pretty,
but we can be in fantastic shape
and can shoot a quick jab to the ribs,
against a background of orange and yellow streamers,
to put your thinking in perspective.
You see, most of us do not use our backs properly,
they float unused in the body's sea,
retreat like flights of steps into the earth,
or mount birds and hurtle through space
in a universe of misuse —

a setting of deserted and elaborate terrain.
Other things happen during my lifetime;
cotton, for example, becomes a less important product,
although it remains an inviting mass of clouds.
The wallpaper of NYU surrounds my present responsibilities,
wheeling Rachel through Washington Square Park,
but I can see through them
to some azure cows mooing in a yellow country sky.

Or a label covers part of its bottle, simple enough,
and by itself
can hold the language back one single minute
from the metaphoric abyss.

Or a girl comes to the door and means to widen her eyes.
Hand her a crust of bread and return to your work,
a note to Charles North,
a note to Sylvia Plath,
and a yellow phial filled with cloudy fluid;
I spent a lot of time on it, thinking about it,
changing it again in a quiet rage, spilling it,
soaking it back up with a sponge,

and by this time everyone is in stitches.
On a smaller scale, a puddle is covered over with boards
and an awning shields several successful men from the sun.
I know none of this is really true,
until the damned car ran over the embankment,
which was also not true;
hundreds of wheels,
and the embankment the diamond border of another state,
and the road a river stretching far to the west,
and along the way slopes leading down beneath the trees,
and from there the clearing I had seen before
from a silent pool of sunlit air,
looking from this spot and from others
to the same imaginary points among the stars.

The landscape is still very pretty but there are too many people.
There have always been too many people
and they obviously have something in common,
but that's as far as it goes,
a friendly chat or violent debate among civilizations,
comparing pyramids, admiring one another's feathers,

while muskrats keep nibbling the grass
and I prop up my feet on a temporary framework,
and I again open Spenser
and would gallop onto the plains,
a distinguished figure on the back of poetry,
non-ferrous castings holding me securely
to the machinery of composition.
But do not jump to conclusions,
I can be entertaining as well as literate,
as well as thought-provoking and lucid,
reflective and supremely melancholy
after relating the fashionable drolleries of the day;
in short like a newspaper, sealed off from the floor
by the knees of my beloved
and open to her incisive and affectionate perusal.

By the editorial of course she is dozing;
the soup bubbles merrily on the stove,
personalities of tiny fragments, sharply transitional,
parades of figures that die like a mosquito,
slapped against the forehead in a surfeit of imagery,
one minor event and then another,
exaggerated even further during the night,
building up the daily framework until forced to seek revenge
and dying like a dog in the gutter,
installed in the tradition determined by sanitary bliss.
In another picture, if I understand my vision correctly,
Nebraska shines with a burning aura,
and elsewhere in that same picture
it appears again, consumed and glowing quietly,

with shapes nearby not too dissimilar, Colorado, the Dakotas,
with a definite luminosity always from around their borders.
The people back east are dogs, asses, or cats,
sheep, rats, parrots, or pigs.
Out west they are rabbits, bulls, or coyotes,
mice, or low, like snakes. The rest of us are without interest,
trapped like insects within the merely human personality,
huddled together in our rented leaking rooms,
with only the wallpaper to suggest the wrought-iron entranceway,
a passage down the marble hall, the balconies, the stairwell,
and the bow-window of the dining room,
the visit miles away at the bottom of a glass
in a tradition determined by liquid tropical bliss.

I was born in those United States too,
and for a long while it seemed useless,
time pattering by on its iambic feet,
followed sometimes too closely by anapestic ones,
and ultimately stampeded by the thousands of feet
having no proper accent at all, the endless pyrrhic journey
discussed in an English aspiring to the grains of sand,
trampling the literature until it screams with hyperbole,
and generating a confusion unequalled since 1950,
when I stood in the same place in the playground next to my school
and had the same thought I had there the year before
and knew that this was going to occur yet again the following year,
and that then as now the intervening months
will have seemed to have passed in an instant,
and that no matter when I looked back from the future

all the previous years would have flown in a second,
the cartoon with the one perennial frame.

But newspapers do not think and act by themselves,
someone has to get up, bored,
so that I fall to the floor in a heap,
a lowly detail of my own description,
while she walks away like success and failure
and the pages pile up from room to room
until the apartment is an informed but littered mess.

I periodically avoid that reality for a few minutes
by delving into the contrived and picturesque,
the façade of a palace, a cathedral, a lengthening shadow,
a cloud drifting along above
while shaded figures disappear beside the canal,
or rest beneath an unseen melon canopy;
and pieces of rock break off beyond their reach
from a distant cliff;
and their pounding hearts,
as they scatter whispering to their costumes,
passing through a vestibule into a low room.

I pause, and think about the human condition.
I look out at the sky,
which is rich, and brown, like a leaf
floating all the way down to our narrow jungle floor
and becoming like a tiny person during the night
talking in the clichés of our computerized age;

though people were always reduced to numbers
whenever one wanted to count them,
in our case to over 200 million Americans,
and we are counted again for our ethnic identities,
each of us secretly knowing it is the wrong one;
and we do not enjoy our empire,
a claim to historical uniqueness
along with the Bomb,
the scientific equivalent of the Deep Image,
and the morning's sun arises in splendor
to intensify the insane bullshit of time and place.

So *this* is the famous Meadowbrook Parkway at dawn
for example, a dwarf transept in the cathedral of Nassau,
running at once toward the valuable properties on the Sound,
and south to the famous crowds on the beach,
who believe they are wading out toward their ancestral homes
in Europe and Africa,
but who in reality face the remainder of the New World
which soon began to yawn like a professional,
trapped in the craters of the periods and apostrophes,
having been inserted as the second sheet
for the writings of the past.
Another possibility is that the universe is a spoon
of enormous depth,
stirring an infinite cauldron of soup, or a fork
to prod the roasted planets of gas
until they break up in hopeless laughter
and slop over the sides
onto the indivisible floor of night; or it is a ladle,

scattering pinpoints of sensation before your eyes
in an astounding flood of information
greeting you suddenly on your return from a walk.
Indeed, one staggers in, silhouetted against the February sky,
back from a tour of no less than fifty centuries,
to collapse on the bed like all the others.
Indeed, your position can be revealed to the howling mob
of rugged individualists
who become enraged en masse
like a blind spot in the electricity
that shows you at a glance the night as it has always been.

Long before 1950 I knew that one of the numerous years
would bring death, as 1939 brought life,
in the way that two poems on universal themes
open and close an important collection;
or with a novel, its epigraph and after 600 pages —
coming to one's senses and closing it before the last, the 601st,
because there are a host of other good books
to be read, written, and published by far-seeing publishers,
who like the authors themselves are high on the evolutionary scale,
where death is the occasion for great verbosity
which, like vegetables from the Massapequa Market,
imparts a healthy glow.
With Rembrandt, I understand that there is no history,
there is only pride, fury, and frustration
and the glow
these fevered emotions can impart to my work,
applied in phrases built up like brushstrokes,
but apprehended in a sequential structure, like music;

there is very little left for poetry itself,
it is only the core
on which to hang the mountainous array of information,
and which is not gathered from the *anguish* of life, exactly,
although it is that very word that has sometimes shaken my heart,
verging on the French, as have the English always,
two percent (2%) less oriental refinement
due to an arriviste position analogous to Spain's
and two percent (3%) more Teutonic brooding,
due to the raging sea, the barren crags, and deserted fens,
which was why I was resting my head in the first place,
distorting human affairs in the polemics of survival,
in the enigmas posed by the use of the words themselves,
sustaining almost anything that floats.

The lights come back on, in the company of others,
in mediaeval values brought to their modern equivalents.
I pick up a newspaper, and put it back down.
I pick up a tape-measure and start rolling it out,
making a mark at 31 and continuing,
until at 60 it stops altogether
and I look out at the unrecorded distance.
Then I just sit quietly for a while
in a blaze of liquid sensation. Skiing is not allowed,
nor is hunting or fishing,
just gliding along a low cliff for a while, then out above the deep.
I am basically a moderate person and often tire of myself,
my drunken attempts to sum up existence in an evening,
like poetry in that one makes impossible demands of it,
or one can be found differently,

smashed on the sidewalk in a trance, face down,

having imagined some great piece of nonsense from the heights

to permeate the ridiculous ease of existence.

I refill my glass and light a match,

but after that things are at a standstill,

or they skitter away like a muskrat

until expanded into something more exciting

for the entertainment of the great, and politically well-placed,

as well as for those who feel that they sink through a sieve

and who seek an explanation for this.

In our American English is the expression "left field."

It is the largest of the three fields,

and the one Americans most often come from,

walking with limps toward the setting sun.

Really only about one-third of the news they hear

can be considered "bad"; and of that

an even smaller percentage which could be called truly disastrous,

or "catastrophic," in the classic sense;

but when one brings up the subject of poetry,

discharging it among minor globules of conversation,

they shiver up the length of their spines.

They know that millions have died horribly from excessive reading,

useless quotations trickling from parched and swollen throats,

closing glassy eyes directed in vain

to a final mirage of feeble verse

overwhelmed by relief columns of practical industriousness,

an assault even on the dreams of my great predecessors,

Generals Grant and Washington,

who fell and died with a splash in the poetic lake of their country,
which is no worse than having noodles for brains, or ice cream.

Like religion, I cannot agree,
I simply admonish.
I operate in a prescribed area,
from one end of a spectrum to another.
I fall in a heap sometimes,
on your doorstep in a bundle,
spilling out in any number of ways;
and missing many opportunities,
some of which do not yet really exist;
as visitors over two miles away, on Maple Avenue,
a street over two miles away,
and during the journey the moods are sharply transitional,
almost a parody of Shakespeare as one scene relieves another,
and in almost all of them are moments of crisis.

Hmm. Change and growth, stagnation and decay.
With other devices I circle the rooftops.
I burst onto the scene, mature by 1848,
and settle down to the gourmandise of Victorian inelasticity.
Below stairs, in the kitchen, there is related a classic metaphor,
in which an iron ladle of universal night
scatters a trail of visibly glowing stars
across the artistically morbid nineteen-fifties,
determined by people molded in the Twenties,
enduring the artistic spasms of their maturity.
I finish reading *The French Lieutenant's Woman*,
and wish that Charles would end up with Sarah.

TONY TOWLE

That's what the Fifties were all about,
ending up with the right person,
as opposed to with God or the Apocalypse,
which would be very difficult for me to comprehend,
but very interesting.

I start off the Seventies, publish a book, and fall back exhausted,
to languish in my personal version of the ex-neo-Protestant ethic,
although I am not really competent to speak of it,
nor would it be in good taste.
For my part I just take it or leave it,
like November on the leg of the needle's quadrennial plunge,
when political famine rages
and Wit is burned in the presence of Theory,
with a bowl of warm and bloody water as a side dish;
when the electorate acts *automatically*,
in that is has "no effect" on the rest of the year;
while I shun the crowds like a person from the Fifties
and autumn turns peacefully to winter
and your hair descends in sudden glory,
as on the soft shoulders of the daily epic,
which gets pushed roughly down at the close of day
for the crude pleasure of its simple narrative;
a train grinds to a halt, for example, a man emerges
holding a sealed and grimy box; the box is resealed,
I awaken, and the man returns by car.

But the lyric as well ends up more or less prone
on the rumpled bed of narration,
summer turning peacefully to autumn, for example,

as a few flakes of rust float allegorically onto the highway,
while I look out at the afternoon sun,
having arisen again from the cold June water.
On a pure whim I get up and pour out a drink, three fingers,
and then another,
with puzzling but gratifying effects;
I visit Rome for the first time, and Greece, old women
carrying candlesticks and not without prejudice,
who soon have you munching garlic and stale bread,
hauling their barrels up from the Mediterranean,
getting stains on your picturesque clothing,
and suffering the insolence of the northern peoples
in their idiot perpetual renaissance,
onions falling out of a bag.

I crawl back through the sawdust to my table,
searching for a perfect phrase. I sit down
and begin the American epic,
in which gods and goddesses in the late 18th century
sprinkle the dust of adventurous enlightenment
on a passing eagle,
who lands as if on vacation and beats the dust into rebellion,
flecked with the vestigial droplets of Puritanism,
the vestigial mediaeval reaction
to the sensual abandon of Renaissance curiosity.
The God of War enters with a sword;
I run forward with a pen and tell him to leave.
Greatly incensed, he leaves with his attendants,
his brazen shield indelibly spotted with the ink of truth.
So you see it is possible, from my experience,

TONY TOWLE

to rout the forces of war and disruption,
who become like straying sheep,
and borrow a woman's skirt and bonnet
(which they sometimes forget to return)
and play some domestic comedy involving food:
bread, corn, beans, and steak,
the odds and ends of a homely American cooking
eaten by men who grumble and women who lament,
as curtains lower to the familiar smells of frying potatoes,
onions, and rice;
a performance ending up not so much as a *nocturne*
but a NOCturn, the first syllable getting most of it over with,
so that with the brief appearance of the final syllable
one can merely retire to a convenient flat rock
and watch the sun move on in its fate,
through one transparent door after another,
leaving them open for us to follow after
in the subordinate madness of a satellite.

It is in that vein, then, the rich streaming blood of comedy,
that I shoot the rapids,
the humorlessness of the turbulent times in which I live,
and plunge over the falls
and pierce the ripe giant tomato of death,
and continue in its vast red pulp at last truly alone.
I fall to dozing about it,
and occasionally try to write about it,
and then stop, as if for a nap.
I tried last winter in "Sleep and Poetry,"
at the end awakening, as if from a nap.

Then as now my life is very simple and of course tragic,
but my thoughts are very complicated.
I had always found my thinking inexplicable
and then, on July 15, 1960, I began writing poems,
which oddly enough has made me feel gradually more comfortable,
at least an improvement over when I was nine, in Rego Park,
slowly ripening beside the great asphalt ladle of Queens Boulevard
which led a broad trail of starry lights
to the distant elegance of a visible Manhattan,
which proved still to be there after many years, August 1960,
when I returned in anonymous triumph to the island of my birth.

Next door, back in Rego Park at the end of the Forties,
"Walden Terrace" arose, its eight stories of cement
making obsolete our previously majestic six of brick,
and was the home of Sid Caesar for a while
who was good for a dollar tip on a drugstore delivery.
People came from nowhere after the war,
like going nowhere during it.
We played in the postwar expansion as the buildings went up,
then faced with a vanished frontier our families pushed on,
out to the Island, to Jersey, or Connecticut;
mine trekked to the silver Alaska of Westchester,
to picturesque Dobbs Ferry on the imposing Hudson,
where you got beaten up if you were Jewish,
far from the recently victorious Israeli army,
and where the devout Irish mayor taught public high school as well,
and was the scourge of the Protestant students.

TONY TOWLE

The lethargic Hudson gleamed in the sun,
symbolizing our forthcoming journey into the world,
as the nearby ruins of the Jay Gould estate were the window
on man's glory and predictable fall.
By 1953, "Ferry" was one of those inescapable puns.
Popular music was terrible.
Many of the people who I saw on those streets
have died in the meantime, complaining bitterly, et cetera,
part and parcel of the last hundred years,
which like the last five have been a period of transition,
demonstrably different at the extremes,
but with many of the same people alive for a good deal of it,
until each dies, finally, closing the transparent door in front of us,
and like the dawn is a symbol for progress and a new beginning,
an elderly man, who enters for a moment to give some sound
        advice.
Like Walden Terrace it is usually cement,
leading like a path from the back door to the garage,
and then a long drive down a deserted highway
past a setting for something very real,
like Elvis Presley in 1957,
closing the door behind you in much the same way,
taking the dog out for a walk and coming back in for dinner.

More often, though, one's life and times speak for themselves,
poured out before you from a sparkling ladle of expectations,
the physical abstractions I wash in and walk through,
working hard to relax in them,
closing my eyes on the roof of the world,

rain turning to snow, removed from the company of others,
and by the time it melts everything has changed.

More truthfully, on feeling the first few drops
I just go inside,
make a few phone calls and then hang up,
after having described exactly the way I see things,
which is in a glare,
but more the glare of the south and its blue treacherous coast,
not the staggering lonely white glare of the far north,
where eventually you stumble into the arms of a bear
and give up, in a dazzling flurry of blood and fur.
But there is another option, the middle way,
the temperate zone on the eastern coast,
a smoldering environment of temptation and betrayal,
immersed in the cauldron of boiling anticipations,
sitting on what appears to be an empty stage
bathed by an emblematic moon.
Furtive silhouettes enter from stage right and stage left,
monstrous allies of dubious organization,
gliding up the aisles where you shiver with fright,
until you knock the plugs out and they stiffen with cold.
After the harmful liquid has drained,
you stroll at random among the limp and soggy items,
to find something useful for poetry; much as a dermatologist
ironically would search for healthy skin, grimace, and move on.

There are other specialists in the fields of literature,
almost too numerous to mention,
except through a few cryptic references

set within lush imagery and sparkling observations,
and in between the great saga of America,
lying like a lost nickel in New York's platonic gutter,
or found in one of the real ones
existing platonically for years in my vision of New York,
which has proved still to be here after all this time,
bathed in the artifice of the nightly moon.
When it becomes too completely real
I may jump far out into the night,
to be lifted up by a great starry ladle,
and spooned into the cauldron of infinity.

Perhaps you are being prodded by these culinary figures
into the beginnings of an appetite,
and the rest of the poem
begins to rise up like the Andes, before which
you have been forced inconveniently to camp this evening,
and in the chill dawn you find that nothing has changed,
staring at the ashen embers and the cold cup of oily coffee
and the peaks loom upwards still,
and you begin to hallucinate a warm hearth and steaming gravy
spooned over succulent morsels of roasted meat.

The image will have to keep for a while
in the luxurious bubble of your imagination,
for there is the inexorable winter of these final hundred lines,
hard, uneven ground, impossible for trucks or horses,
on which, in their version of the Middle Ages,
Europeans searched for firewood,
using the leftovers to build some ships

for sailing out and finding empires;
studying feverishly, arranging for transportation,
hiring mercenaries; the banter is very loud;
people's lives in general are far from private,
and in two senses — the part that is determined to rise,
and the part that is discovered as a vehicle
for moving along the ground, nettles along for the ride
on the corpulent coachman's tattered coat.
I sit back to enjoy the ride,
my head a veritable brimming cask, a flickering distant campfire
in the relentless flow of night.
Its blackness can limit our activities
but not our restless thoughts,
rendering the dark in dialect
and wending their way through space.

I turn out the lights and get into bed,
the forces of gravity holding me in place
on the wrinkled skin of the earth.
In general our underlying materials must improvise constantly
to refresh their jaded covering fabrics.
The interior of the universe itself
consistently pokes and arouses its translucent wrapping
which on every side must face the unknown.
I get out of bed and go to the store,
observed and alone like the educated suburbs.
I open a book but fail to read it,
turn out the lights and toss in my bed.
I talk a great deal but it is not the truth,
it is an intellectual shorthand, like painting and music

TONY TOWLE

and it goes on into the night.
I stumble out in the night, turn around
and come back in the morning,
my nebulous dialect keeping its distance,
awaiting the dreaded delivery up to the typewriter,
distorted beyond recognition in floods of internal description,
jumbled with pieces from books and from music,
the surface of painting, sculpture, and prints
which momentarily sweep from the mind its trivia
and which all together fill an immense goblet
from which I drink by definition in failing health
as much as can be held;
and for that informative time
spreading out as far as possible into the infinite,
no more than a few miles really,
until I feel more peculiar than usual.
I break the ice and plunge into bottomless sleep.
I lie in bed and think about life
or get up and go to the store,
taking a tentative step on the soft pear of convention
which can lead to sinking into the worst of two worlds,
the world of fashion and the world of bitter hallucination,
where crisis, pain, and emptiness color the imagination —
miles of crystalline glacier,
shafts of sunlight and the haunted fields.

I gallop onto the plains,
a distinguished figure on the back of poetry.
I relax my vigilance, raise the blind
and observe the sky.

I verge on the maudlin, jump the gun, drag my ass,
have a quick Pernod with other poets,
reach for the sky, turn the screw, and fall out —
take a powder and hang it up.
I venture into the unknown.
I play by the rules, branch out,
and stay in my place.
I walk into the wind, continually,
have lunch on velvet burgundy tablecloths with friends,
dress for dinner in elegant striped jackets,
or fabulous gray suits,
a pestilent green hat or short furry slippers,
fashion with charm like the perennial sea
in that it is always pulling at your leg,

or concocting a simple soup.
I enter another year, 1973. I read Verlaine,
feel my pulse and drink some rum,
take some shit, bust some balls and run like hell,
until sleep-inducing herbs permeate the room
from an odiferous panel, or cylinder.
The sugar softens in my coffee;
I outwear my welcome, always,
harnessed like a horse to a tale,
casting about in an endless mire,
along with the other poets, my worthy opponents,
flying for hours and then some relaxation,
between the sky and the ground,
in our purely hypothetical space.

TONY TOWLE

Epilogue

Nothing will happen here, now, to you,
something will happen later;
a story has a beginning and an end,
ambitions and limitations,
and some scientific proof.
It bears you finally downward,
through mysterious questions
to unpleasing answers,
over the warm ground and in driving rain,
the mind shedding pages like the trees,
the stars of imagination in eclipse,
growing in richness and ingenuity,
the sparkling glimmer of communities.

Social Poem

It's six o'clock, do you know
where you are? I am with my sanity
among the bells
telling me it is six o'clock,
which is more than I need to know.

I seem to want to talk about something,
but it is missing,
which makes it a personal remark
which I stop to listen to
as if the bells had stopped ringing
but I were persisting
as if the walls were further away
than just on the other side,
as the interior floods
with the gloom of the typewriter
and I memorialize a pond
stirred by fish through ugly shadows
I have to make use of. Actually
I am upset
with my tone of voice,
as if I had climbed the walls
but did not get far enough away,
though in the first place
I don't know where that would be
and in the second
I know everything else,
which leads to too much news. Maybe

the walls aren't even there anymore,
since nothing seems to be there anymore,
as if the present were an elaborated ambush,
the finale instead of the usual ambience
until a later hour.
And I haven't even gotten to sociability yet,
grasping at its details
and freeing them like peasants
to a thimbleful of history.
Why a thimble? My jacket
needs a button,
but that isn't what I mean by traveling,
I mean that one should be somebody else
and actually go,
although I am somebody else
and have stayed; still living and walking
near Spring Street,
though when I observed it first
there wasn't its bar
accommodating the many people who came from the distance
and got used to me, filtered from the past —
which doubles as much of the day.
And I still cross Houston Street
in the path of the many drivers from New Jersey
who I am sure are all nice people
when they get back; but in the meantime
they are after me,
since I don't mind being paranoid;
it is no worse than riding off into a joke
that of course I would not understand,

lost in generalizations,
and filtered through metaphysical situation
onto geographical surface,
where I am thinking about Jackson Pollock
for some reason,
the rumors and rectangles
from the Cedar Bar to the Metropolitan, the legend
half of me would like the other half to be,
though if I could say which half were which
I wouldn't get any further;
but the real joke is I don't have a horse,
so that crossing Houston Street is truly pedestrian,
which might be good for the paranoia
but not for the legend
I'll be nearer to the next time I stop
at the next place I'll be.

Recapitulation

Wild Assyrian armadillos
couldn't drag me from this place. Just stop it! Just
stop that kind of talk! The music builds,
and raises the lid, until it is off.
Jean's cousin is sleeping over tonight, which I mention
because I seem to be in a different literary tradition tonight,
sort of a "Write 'til you puke" school, though that would probably
take longer than it should; anyway, I continue: Jean is painting,
small canvases, and I am writing, small poems, and I have both a
    glass
of wine and a glass of rum — why limit yourself
if people think you're an alcoholic, in the important
decisions? Part of an incredibly complicated dream I had last night
was that Jean went out and bought cough drops, an incredibly
    ordinary
fact, considering that she has a cough. "Camels," I say, and point
    out
that when Frank, Frank O'Hara, gave up Camels for Marlboros
    back in '64
or was it '65, he lost most of his cough pretty quick but of course
    little
good that did him; I mean it wasn't what did him in. Part
of *Jean's* dream last night, or so she told me and why
should she lie about it, was that I had invited Joe and Eunice Fearer
and Joe and Marjorie Singer to Jean's grandmother's
house in Chicago, with whom I don't get along, the grandmother not
the house and the city falling somewhere in between; I guess the
    reason

the Singers and the Fearers were there is that they recently bought
prints from us, though Jean knows them hardly at all but I've
known them for years; and in addition to this, in the dream, Jean
was introduced to someone who turned out to be someone else, who
then sat down next to her on the sofa and had it out, jerking off,
trying to *come* on her, and I was there too, apparently, and was being
absurdly nonchalant about it, which is maybe in the right direction
    but that
would be beyond even me; far beyond, like these iris vinyl place mats
I'm nowhere near ordering, though if *you're* interested, they're four-
    fifty each
and 18 by 12 — inches — metrics haven't really caught on yet, at least
with *my* particular poetic self: "And kilometers and kilometers to go
before I watch TV…" There are no doubt other reasons
why that one doesn't work, but there's no point in criticizing
my own materials, since someone else is almost sure to. At
Ted Greenwald's wedding not too long ago I opined, or, rather,
asked rhetorically (I thought) what would become of the New York
School of Poetry (having noticed a number of the other guests) if
somebody blew up the building (probably someone who hadn't been
invited) and a colleague within earshot said, or opined, that it would
be improved. Now, eliminating the building as a possibility for "it,"
    "it"
occurred to me that my own work was included in this appraisal,
but on the other hand he was also including his own, which was both
self-effacing and, at the same time, again considering the guests,
more eclectic than the implications of my original remark; but since
the building *didn't* blow up I am here thanking you for your
    patience and

cooperation. I would never let a mere *appraisal* stop me anyway
    (though
a small-caliber revolver would probably do the trick). The wine
is beginning to taste acidic, I'll stick to the rum, while Jean
is still painting and while her cousin, Martha by name, is
    presumably
asleep, and while the television carries on with its endless
    entertainment
and the music indicates that Frederic March's wife is dying.

Another Zone (Prelude)

In the end you take off from your former world,
the rambunctious wings folded in for the day,
the smoky air settling down over the brushwork,
the whole treated to my casual but gregarious inaccuracies,
with imperfections for the entire family:
the reviewers and the reviewed,
the editors and the edited, all the wretched of the earth
at its flattest, the wretched page,
which has now ripened, ever so slightly,
into the details of time and place, land and sea,
brightly seductive, or somber, ill-lit, and grave
and looking for a few more good words
to fill out the diminishing weeks,
the weekly reversals of the Christian tradition:
coming alive on Friday and dying on Sunday
against a background of lawns and coffeepots, steaks and spaniels,
which was nothing like the original cartoon,
once you clean off the dirt with some turp,
which was of a moose chasing a kind of weasel with a two-by-four,
or something,
but anyway the merest sketch
when a thickly crowded panorama
pushing across the bridge of evolution
would have done just as well;
but I'm going back upstairs
and look out the window of America,
which I thought somebody was supposed to clean once in a while,
not that it would change the view:

TONY TOWLE

pastel sunset landscapes sinking into the western foam,
where I would fly like a common bird
and get away from the Cask-of-Amontillado number
the buildings in architectural agglomerations
pull on you here in Downtown New York;
but no island is an island
if you duck your head far enough beneath the waves
and observe the microscopic connections
and listen to the complaints of the sunken travelers,
their obscured vocabulary standing out from the rest of the bullshit,
and we obtusely concentrate on the former
when the latter would do just as well.
I too saw this day a pretty street
and I scrape the clarion layers of paint from the walls
and find stationary shadows on the layers beneath;
it's one more scenario I've got to think up feelings for
at some point — but a snail with a limp could go faster than this,
and since I no longer have so much time
that's all for the prose. For poetry,
the dawn comes up and I make some more coffee,
and it awakens me to the whispering
of yet ten *more* turbulent years,
and I drink the coffee,
and wait for someone to believe me,
the rain not yet having reached the ground,
and I jump toward the sun
that still reaches to this moment,
the sun the same messenger, Guillaume Apollinaire,
it's all still the same, August 26, 1989.

The Art of War

I'm sorry I was asleep when you called.
I was up 'til dawn
attacking the Prussians at *Ligny*,
and I didn't do a good job, I'm afraid, there
were still plenty left
when I pushed "save"
and shut down the computer. I'm glad
I didn't know any of them personally
as I ordered the 12-pounders
to concentrate on the tiny clusters of veteran brigades,
and clicked on all the available cavalry
to erase the inexperienced *Landwehr* from the screen.

TONY TOWLE

Scenario

Memo: wander the streets of Rome endlessly,
until, tired of your foreign misimpressions,
a troop of *Bersaglieri*
takes your imagination off on a brisk trot
to the Castel Sant'Angelo,
where they have not had an execution for a long time
but seem willing, now, to restart the tradition.
"I have captured your imagination," asserts the *Intendente*
of subconscious rambling, and the sun and the moon unite
to dribble gold and silver down the bib of the executioner;
and the ax does fall
but is just one more unrecorded incident
taking place in my head in a bar near Canal Street,
Angelo's, where bar-stool inertia has set in,
a scene within a faded reproduction within foliate carving
of Violi's great canvas, *Canal Street*,
hanging dim and baroque above the customers.
Indeed, morsels of roast swan
are all that's left on the steam table,
and so in the picture I remain hungry,
making do with gratuitous details,
such as the pair of snow leopards
who wait to escort me to my blind date,
a 2500-year-old Scythian princess,
who I hope will be thawed and animate
by the time I call at her tomb of logs
high in the Altai Mountains;
and the bouquet I bring swirls

with the kitsch of autumn colors,
and silvery moonbeams dance about,
and I was sure I could stay there, quiet,
and partake of that vista forever,
time stopping allegorically in its tracks ¾
but then comes the call to action, to get up;
with a few artful taps from the hammer of creativity
I'm on my way, a dancing moonbeam.

Ethos

Vous êtes un de ces types Protestants qui
se trouve seulement à Genève
(You are one of those Protestant types
one finds only in Geneva)
I overheard an older man saying lasciviously to a young one
at the Cedar Bar a very long time ago
in clear, textbook French and I was startled,
apprehensive for a second that it had been directed at me,
though I have never been to Geneva —
and I don't think that's what Calvin had in mind
when *he* went to Geneva; he went to create an ethos,
through which as a distant subtextual consequence
I find myself engaged in marginally necessary yardwork
somewhere between Olivebridge and Krumville
to justify midnight sensuality later on,
in the waters of the enchanted spring
with *Dian*, the woodland nymph
who conveyed me here from the metropolis
by means of a spirited white Toyota.
But work for reward is not what Calvin meant either,
really, yet it is out of his control, isn't it,
for that's what happens to an ethos: it dapples the landscape
like invisible confetti from a distant century,
falling unobserved as one rakes the leaves,
gathers the kindling.

Bagatelle

Clouds have again
seized control of the weekend
and Teshub, storm god of the Hittites
(Toshiba, according to the SpellCheck)
casually mentions, in a moistened Aramaic
(which is odd, because it is not
his first language, nor
as you might suppose, is it mine)
that we're really in for it this time,
that *liquidity* will be a daily
fact of life for the rest of the year
which means, he explains, that in addition
to the endless rain, cosmic investors
could turn in our world to make a profit
at the planetary exchange —
or more likely to cut a loss.
Since I have already removed the helmet of judgment
I should check on the proceedings in Orange County
where "Tony Towle" is suing David M. Reyneaud,
et al. for automotive negligence. It seems
Dave and those other bastards out there
tried to run down the last persona
I can afford to maintain in Southern California,
my liquidity being what it is,
not that he ever provides any interesting imagery —
just sits on the beach all day and stares at the ocean
in a vast impression of liquidity,
a Mr. Hulot's Holiday without the verbosity,

which is exactly the kind of reference
that sails right over his head and plunks into the Pacific
and that he thinks must have been a fish.
By now I'm on a trip, if not exactly a vacation
though I am expecting brambles, mosquitoes,
poisonous berries and lunatics with shotguns
as I usually encountered on vacation,
except when I would sit on the beach
and consider the Great North Atlantic,
investing the feeling
that vacations would last longer
than I knew they were going to. But it seems Teshub,
as is the way with storm gods, was hyperbolizing
for the rain has finally stopped;
Apollo has opened another referential window
and is beginning to apply sunlight to the moisture.
"Have a swell apotheosis," Teshub tells me
and, startled, before I can manage a "Thanks, you too"
we are parted by the clearing air.

Seven-O (Toasts)

To the long stretches of time
of paying little attention
to what might be going wrong inside—
farewell. And here's
to the restoration of cause
in its ratio to irascibility
to something more than absolute zero.
As for the growing assemblage of pills,
I take heart in the words of the Earl of Rochester to Charles II:
I mean really, Sire, if we couldn't wash down
our Atenolol and Coumadin
with a decent Châteauneuf-du-Pape,
what the devil would be the point of going on?

And although I don't have to answer that question just *yet,*
there are many more things I could drink to
than my capacity these days can support,
so we'll take a break
with some mental acuity exercise:

Can *you* find the Prussian General Staff of 1870 in this waterfall,
for example, or discern Stalin's intentions toward the *kulaks*
in the rosebush in the foreground?
Note the charming antique armoire in spiced pine
sinking slowly into the marsh; without your glasses,
determine on which still-visible drawer the grain is closest
to the topographic map of the state in which you were born.
Finally, before we move on, see if you can locate the golf ball,

TONY TOWLE

a *Titleist 1* with a nick in it,
hit 50 years ago that ended up in the pond—it made a *sploosh*
by the way, and thus ended its wayward journey with a digraph.
Golf Balls in the Pond is an elevating
album of verse about personal loss
that I no longer have time enough to read—or to write,

either. I wonder what percentage of my life has been spent
trying to be funny and ending up otherwise.
The number is somewhere in the waterfall.
And here's to keeping it ambiguous enough
for the universe to suspend my fate
until it shakes the dust from a billion suns, at least.

LIFE

Photo Credit: David Kelley, 1990

TONY TOWLE

I first met Tony Towle in the spring of 2003 at the Fish Bar in the East Village, in Manhattan. My first impression was of an opinionated man in his mid-to-upper sixties who walked with a cane. (He has used a cane since 1997, as a result of slipping on a patch of ice in 1991, and also due to an undiagnosed neurological condition.) His beard was well trimmed and his gray hair parted neatly to the side. His glasses hung from a chain around his neck, and he wore a button-down Oxford, a pair of worn jeans and gray athletic shoes. I heard that he was something of a lady's man when younger, and had been a much heavier drinker. I went to the Saint Mark's Bookshop soon after and flipped through his chapbook Nine Immaterial Nocturnes *(2003). I was immediately struck by the imagery—such as the final lines of "Ethos": "for that's what happens to an ethos: it dapples the landscape / like invisible confetti from a distant century, / falling unobserved as one rakes the leaves, / gathers the kindling." Tony was initially wary about my book, explaining that the psychological treatments of poets he'd read tended to "ransack" the life to expli-cate the poems, whereas poetry, for him, was, if not outside of life exactly, only coincidentally autobiographical.*

EARLY HISTORY

The gulls glide, in 1939, into the bonus of another country,
the balloons and machinery of all the Europes and
    Americas,
a hundred million thoughts at rest in the river,
stirring, as I begin to think about myself,
and in the history of my ears making a beginning of the
    frontier.

        —*from* "Sunrise: Ode To Frank O'Hara" (1966–67)

Tony Towle was born into a middle-class family in 1939 at Lenox Hill Hospital in Manhattan. The Towles lived in Inwood before moving to Rego Park in Queens when he was two, so his father, who did non-aviation interior design work for American Airlines, could be closer to the airport that would be LaGuardia. They lived on the top floor of a six-story brick building off the ten-lane thoroughfare of Queens Boulevard, looking west toward Manhattan. There were twenty such buildings, new at the time, in a two-block complex. By the time the Towle family moved into Apartment 6D at 64–39 98th Street, in 1941, the area was poised to become a fast-growing white middle-class neighborhood, which became increasingly Jewish over the next decade. Their apartment building was the last before several block-long, deep excavations stretching west that had been put on hold during World War II and which provided Tony and his friends overgrown vacant lots to spend long afternoons playing in. These lots did not resume development until a couple of years after the war. Here's how Tony describes Rego Park in the long poem "Autobiography," from 1970–73:

Next door, back in Rego Park at the end of the Forties,
"Walden Terrace" arose, its eight stories of cement
making obsolete our previously majestic six of brick,
and was the home of Sid Caesar for a while
who was good for a dollar tip on a drugstore delivery.
People came from nowhere after the war,
like going nowhere during it.
We played in the postwar expansion as the buildings went
   up,
then faced with a vanishing frontier our families pushed
   on. . .

Tony characterizes his childhood—at least up to the age of ten or so—as "imaginative" and "escapist." He recalls that the apartment buildings on his block were connected on the rooftops and through labyrinthine basement passageways that felt like a subterranean maze. His childhood memories reflect an awareness that "the city" (Manhattan) was "over there," a distant skyline. Quoting again from "Autobiography,"

. . . . .on July 15, 1960, I began writing poems,
which oddly enough has made me feel gradually more
   comfortable,
at least an improvement over when I was nine, in Rego
   Park,
slowly ripening beside the great asphalt ladle of Queens
   Boulevard
which led a broad trail of starry lights
to the distant elegance of a visible Manhattan...

Although he has a vague recollection that he could see Manhattan in the distance from his bedroom window, his father, who was an artist as well as interior designer, had stylized paintings of New York's skyscrapers hanging in the apartment, as well as framed Museum of Modern Art reproductions of Matisse's *The Young Sailor II*, an O'Keeffe "Barn," and Picasso's *Three Musicians*. Of course he didn't know these titles or who the artists were, or that they were "reproductions," until many years later.

He tells of a very early memory of wearing a pair of striped overalls that were ridiculed by an older child in the apartment complex's playground. (He realized about ten years ago, when he discovered family photographs in which he was *wearing* these striped overalls, that he was three years old at the most.) He also remembers drawing caricatures of Hitler and Mussolini and Tojo on oblong wooden blocks; and the Victory Garden plot his mother kept during the war in the block-long lot on which Walden Terrace was later built. Tony grew up hearing the sound of constant traffic on Queens Boulevard from his bedroom, punctuated by the periodic silences provided by red lights. He thinks that it was for this reason that his first visit to the country, at the age of five or so, was frightening. The "deafening silence" and "dark tree shapes I could see out the window" were scary, as was the realization that anyone could just come through the window anytime. His bedroom in Rego Park, after all, was a good fifty feet off the ground.

Tony's father, Erwin Weible Towle, was born in 1905 and came from "a somewhat prominent family" in Omaha. His Uncle Roy was elected mayor of the city for a term in the '30s and had also been police chief. The black sheep of the family, Erwin rebelled against Midwestern Protestant values and moved east to New York City at thirty.

Though his college education was intermittent, he had artistic talent and found regular employment as an interior designer and draftsman. Tony characterizes his father as "funny and charming to friends and outsiders," though ambivalent about having a family, insensitive, and absentee. However, Tony credits his father for providing an atmosphere of taste, which, besides the artwork mentioned above, included genuine antiques—a Korean chest, a bronze Buddha, a real Persian rug, Chinese porcelain, and elegant drapes and furniture. His father also had a collection of classical 78s that included Gershwin, Khachaturian, Prokofiev, and Stravinsky. To this day, he remembers the scariness of the album cover of the latter's *Firebird*, seen at the age of four or five. The music itself was a little scary as well. Such twentieth-century classical pieces became his favorites by the time he was a young adult and, with the addition of Bartok, Debussy, Ravel, and Poulenc, among others, have remained so.

Tony's mother, Mary Elizabeth Rigg, was born in 1913 in Decatur, Illinois, and died in 1965 when Tony was twenty-six. His affection for her was obvious by the quiver in his voice when he spoke of her death from cancer. His father died 23 years later, in 1988. At that point he was living in government-assisted housing on Miami Beach. I asked how it was to lose his father and Tony explained, again, that they were never particularly close and that that he didn't travel to Florida to attend the funeral. He was closer to his mother than his father and had a close relationship with his sister, Terry, who was born in 1947 and died of cancer in 1987. The two younger siblings are very much younger: Tom (born in 1954) and Peg (born in 1956). They were placed into foster care as a result of his father's inability to raise them on his own, after his wife died, and Tony regretted not doing more for them at that time.

Tony's feelings for girls were strong but tempered by shyness and insecurity. He had two innocent, romantic relationships in grade school: Maureen in the third grade and, in the fifth, Vibeke, a Danish girl whose father, as he remembers it, worked at the United Nations. (Actually, this was before the U.N. complex was completed.) He recalls spending the 8th grade at the all-boys YMCA McBurney School on 63rd Street and Central Park West in Manhattan. In *Memoir 1960–1963*, he writes, "It was my one year in private school and I had to commute on the subway from Rego Park. It was a boy's school only and, as socially backward a thirteen-year-old as I was, I found that I greatly missed the presence of girls in the classroom." When his family moved to Dobbs Ferry the following year, he attended a public (co-ed) high school but didn't have a girlfriend until his sophomore year when he went out with a classmate named Roslyn and subsequently lost his virginity. He recalls that she gave him an atlas as a birthday present, in recognition of his interest in geography, history, and for having an "international outlook."

Tony had pored over historical maps back in Queens and read European and world history—especially military history—far beyond what was required for school. He read Froissart's *Chronicles of the Hundred Years' War* when he was nine, which he believes was a delayed inspiration from seeing Laurence Olivier's movie version of *Henry V* at Radio City Music Hall in 1946, which his mother took him to for his birthday. It was a wartime film and Olivier emphasized the military aspect of Shakespeare's play, including a fairly realistic Battle of Agincourt. Tony was fascinated that there had been a "15th Century" and was inspired by the movie's historical aspect. Before long he found that he had knew a great number of historical names and dates, most of which he hasn't forgotten. He feels that knowing dates provides an important framework through which to look at both the past and the present.

By high school, these interests were providing an escape from a present he characterized as "often depressing," perhaps largely because he had no idea of what the future would hold, and what he would do with himself. Regarding writing, he appreciated and had a feeling for the plays and sonnets of Shakespeare that were assigned in class, but, in those days, poetry in his English classes stopped at Longfellow and Tony had no interest in writing any. "It would not have been considered a 'normal' thing for teenage boys to do in the '50s," he remarked; but, aside from the stigma, the thought never occurred to him.

Tony eventually broke up with Roslyn after his family moved to Eastchester in 1956. When he was a senior at his new high school, he started dating a junior, Monica Collins. In the summer of 1957, Monica discovered that she was pregnant, which was inopportune because Tony had been accepted by Georgetown University's School of Foreign Service. A year younger than Tony, Monica dropped out of school and followed the young man whose baby she was carrying to Washington, D.C. They decided to keep the pregnancy secret. Not surprisingly, the situation necessitated that Tony drop out of Georgetown (after only a semester) and find a job. The country was entering a recession, and he had no skills or credentials. He writes in *Memoir* about a job he took in desperation, selling encyclopedias door to door. One evening around Christmas he was left off in a suburban neighborhood in northern Virginia "steeped in despair and self-pitying ruminations, not having come even close to making a sale."

Monica gave birth at Georgetown Hospital to a girl they named Melissa Ann, but there were complications. The baby developed hydrocephalus, or water on the brain, a few days after they brought her home from the hospital. This condition wasn't easily treated in the late '50s. Furthermore, Tony, only eighteen, was not allowed legally to give permission for the operation the doctors at the hospital wanted to perform. Now he had to send a telegram to his parents in Rye, to get them to send long-distance authorization to the hospital, and at the same time admit what the reason was for his and Monica's elopement. They sent the permission, but then the hospital didn't perform the operation after all, since the hydrocephalus had stopped on its own.

It soon became clear that the child would need special care, so the young parents applied to an institutional home for disabled children located in the District of Columbia, referred to as the "D.C. Home," to have her admitted. It cost the District more per month (Tony remembers that it was 180 dollars) than most people could afford, and each applicant was sat in a "witness chair" in a courtroom presided over by a judge, with the other applicants looking on, while a lawyer for the District grilled the applicant as to how much he could afford. There was no "defense lawyer," so the applicant was on his own. Tony, unintimidated, found himself verbally sparring with the young lawyer, who was not accustomed to dealing with people who spoke English as well as he did. Making $35 a week at the time as a mail clerk, he negotiated a payment of $15 each month toward the care of the child. He found it ironic that, even in this tragic scenario, a reflexive linguistic function took over.

A year later, Monica found out that she was again pregnant. They were married at this point, having located a Presbyterian minister in the District willing to marry them while Monica was carrying Melissa Ann. Tony explains that "It took several agonizing months to find a minister who would perform the ceremony, since we were underage, and parental permission was out of the question, since we didn't tell them why we eloped—as if any reasonable person couldn't have given it a good guess." Their second baby, a boy, whom they named Malcolm Scott, was born on April 6, 1959.

Despite having a healthy son, Tony's spirits would periodically deteriorate, and he experienced several episodes of suicidal thoughts. At one of his many jobs during 1958, he had purchased a revolver from a co-worker for $15, a sum that he could not really afford. Five bullets came with the purchase. It occurred to him later that the absence of the sixth one had to do with the gun's being offered for sale. His rationale to Monica was burglars, but, not surprisingly, she was upset by the firearm's presence. Tony would load the gun and place it in the dresser drawer and Monica would find it and take the bullets out. Tony recalls an argument in the spring of 1960, during which he took the gun from the drawer, put it to his temple, and squeezed the trigger six times in front of a horrified Monica. He tossed the gun on the bed and went out for a long walk. Thrown into a complicated situation at a young age, Tony was desperate for a change.

That May he strolled into a Beat Generation-style coffee house, the kind that had started becoming fashionable everywhere. Though he knew vaguely about Jack Kerouac and Allen Ginsberg, he was far from being a beatnik himself. Still, two important things happened at the café: first, he wrote some lines that could be considered his first poem; and second, he began to consider leaving his domestic situation—feeling that, if he didn't, "something bad was going to happen." Here's how he describes it in *Memoir*:

> I had begun, surreptitiously, writing poems in 1960,
> in Washington, in reaction to and escape from a two-
> and-a-half-year-long teenage marriage that had become

unendurable. Sometime that May, I found myself sitting alone in a Beat-style coffee house, writing down a few lines I felt were a poem. With that experience working on me below the surface, in mid-July, on what seemed at the time an impulse from nowhere, I called in sick to my job of two years at a furniture store, walked over to a park on Wisconsin Avenue near our apartment, and wrote my second and third poems. This was exhilarating and at the same time instantly made my current life seem even more unbearable. That evening I had yet one more horrible argument with my wife, Monica, and a day or two later I moved out and got a room by myself, leaving her with Scott, our infant son. I left the job, too, a week or so later, and by mid-August, with a scant forty dollars to my name, I was on the train to New York. I would stay at my parents' house in Rye, their final move in Westchester, until I reestablished myself somehow. I was impelled to leave the situation I was in. Suicide had often struck me as one alternative, poetry had unexpectedly provided another.

Tony represents the emergence of his early poetic identity in more metaphoric and ironic terms in his long poem *Autobiography*:

> For ten years I have courted the muse,
> through memories and despair, poverty,
> the specters of urban development,
> and the blood of an unbelievable impatience.
>
> At a certain point my imagination began to stir, like boats,
> sitting on a still horizon, moved by a gathering breeze,

torn apart in a tempest,

and by the nerves in the following calm.

At first I boiled the language, like an egg,

the spirit broken at the insufferable hands of sociology,

until at last the ground trembled and broke, like an egg,

and I could imagine filling some small need of literature's

as well as finally, and in a modest way, my own ...

With poetry came a relationship with a young woman by the name of Carol Schleicher, whom he met after he moved out of the apartment he shared with Monica. Tony fell for Carol immediately. They proceeded to have an intense two-week romance. He describes her as "a medium-sized brunette with large brown eyes. She was a year younger than I was, and, though she was also from an un-exotic part of Westchester (White Plains), she struck me as extremely cool. She used the French 'tu piges?'—presumably the equivalent of: 'you dig?' She had smoked marijuana, which she referred to as 'boo.'" Despite the fact that he was "afraid of drugs," Carol thought Tony was cool himself, partly because he knew a little French and had a good accent, but also because he carried a pipe in his belt like a pistol. She also appreciated that he wrote poetry and introduced him to contemporary work by reading from Lawrence Ferlinghetti's *Coney Island of the Mind* in her hotel room one night. She told him about the Abstract Expressionist painters in New York, in particular Willem de Kooning, and the bar they hung out at in the Village, called the Cedar.

Tony began daydreaming about an entirely different kind of life: "Carol engendered in me vague dreams of being with her as a poet in New York, meeting painters, hanging out in bars, and doing interesting and artistic things." But Carol disappeared from his life soon after, leaving a note on the door of her apartment saying that she was off to New York and would be back before long. He never heard from her again.

About three weeks later, Tony convinced himself that he needed to move back to New York, whether he saw Carol again or not. Reflecting upon his decision to leave Monica and Scott in Washington, Tony explained that, "It was perhaps both the most precipitate and necessary decision of my life, as well as the least defensible from a conventional point of view."[1]

NEW YORK CITY

Awake, I move in a doubtful margin.
New York is a cloud. I awaken

and pictures move on the wall.
There is nothing to say;

I am alone with the changing weather
and I made sure I was going to be here.

—Poem (1963)

Tony moved in with his parents in Rye and immediately felt stifled by the need to find a regular 9-to-5 job. His family was ambivalent

---

[1] In Tony's absence, Monica worked for a savings and loan company in D.C. and stayed there for her entire working career. She remarried, eventually divorced, and has for many years lived in Alexandria. Scott, whom Tony would see intermittently, grew up and went to Radford College, spent two years in the Army, married, and also settled in Alexandria. He currently teaches high school in northern Virginia.

at best about his decision to leave Monica and Scott to "be a poet," but it was never openly discussed. He tells an anecdote about showing some work to his paternal grandmother, who was close to eighty and visiting from Omaha: "I brought her a half a dozen or so poems and sat there while she read them. After a few minutes, she remarked matter-of-factly, more to herself than to me: 'I just don't see how you're part of us. I just don't see where you come from.' I had nothing to say in response. I didn't know either."

On the first morning of his job search, he took a train to Grand Central and walked halfway up the stairs of an employment agency on 42nd Street, but was hit by the realization that he didn't want a job, at least none that the agency was likely to offer. He went back down the stairs and started walking south on Fifth Avenue until he reached Washington Square Park. Although he didn't know Greenwich Village well, he knew it was the place to be and walked around until he found a café, which he began visiting regularly, called the Figaro. Similar to the sense of alienation he'd experienced at the beatnik café in D.C., he sensed that those who were really with it at the Figaro knew that he was not one of their number. Forty years later, in a poem called "In The Coffee House," Tony refers to his early days there:

> I should have brought
> something to read
> because I have nothing to do now
> but write, the way I used to
> forty years ago, in the Figaro
> in the Village
> at Bleecker and MacDougal, exhilarated
> by loneliness, poverty, and paralyzing
> indecision, resolutely ignoring the fact

that everyone cool in there
knew that I wasn't —
lost to what was happening
behind the overpriced coffee, 35 cents
for the fuel
to infiltrate oblivion;

and I waited for a girlfriend
and composed jejune little ironies
that I hoped would pass for poems
and I had all the time in the world.

It wasn't long before he decided to find the Cedar, hoping to run into Carol there. But instead of a dynamic gathering of Abstract Expressionist painters and their poet friends sipping cocktails, he stepped into a small, dingy bar with several shady-looking men talking in hushed tones, and he left immediately. "The Cedar," he recalls, "was not an inviting watering hole; you had to work your way into it, and I didn't begin that process until at least a year or so later. As for famous artists, if de Kooning himself had been sitting there, I wouldn't have recognized him; I didn't even know what his paintings looked like."

Gradually, though, some semblance of a professional and social life began to congeal. He found a temp job working at *The Herald Tribune* on West 41st Street, and then a position working as a "distributor" at the Franklin Simon Department Store located at 36th Street and Fifth Avenue, even closer to The Village, where he would often walk after work. He enjoyed the fact that it paid $80 a week and that wearing a suit and tie was required, which he preferred "as it provided a veneer of respectability for my general insecurity."

Around this time he met two ex-CCNY students at one of the Village coffee houses, each of whom owned a motorcycle (BMWs, not Harleys, which they assured him was a very different mind-set). They were funny and bright but had "an alienated drop-out attitude" that involved smoking pot and taking speed, peyote and "a bewildering variety of uppers and downers." Though Tony abstained from drugs (he was still afraid of them), he happily accepted an offer to move in with them on Nelson Avenue in the Bronx. Although it felt liberating to be away from his parents, the conditions on Nelson Avenue were by no means ideal. He remembers the place as "*ur*-bachelor accommodations: not much furniture and no attempt at any sort of housekeeping. The dishes were *never* washed." He wrote some poetry while living there, but never shared it, and was not really happy with the results.

However, he began to read contemporary poetry (he had still read almost none), particularly T.S. Eliot's *The Waste Land and Other Poems*. More than Ferlinghetti's *Coney Island of the Mind*, Eliot's lines (especially from *Ash Wednesday*) stuck with Tony, and he had the perception that *The Waste Land* was personal and lyrical, not the epic poem that the footnotes and the book's introduction claimed it to be. Later in 1961 he was living in one room of a townhouse divided into apartments on West 107th Street. A young woman he was seeing at the time introduced him to a number of classic novels, including *Portrait of the Artist as a Young Man*, *Pride and Prejudice*, *Madame Bovary,* and *The Red and the Black.* On several occasions in *Memoir*, Tony underscores that he came at great literature "from left field"—without having studied it "in an academic setting." This autodidactic period involved "the most disciplined reading I have ever done," Tony recalls, "and it worked. Flaubert, Joyce, Stendhal, and Jane Austen were able to keep me from self-pity and claustrophobia."

(He was laid up in his very small room with a severely sprained ankle when he read these books.)

After changing apartments yet again and being laid off from Franklin Simon, Tony worked in the NYU library stacks as a "runner," which he describes as "demeaning," but circumstances necessitated that he remain at the job because he had no money. He characterizes the winter of 1961 as "nightmarish." He was working a grunt job, had no woman in his life, wasn't eating regularly or particularly well, was drinking too much coffee and smoking too many cigarettes, and suffered through a case of anxiety-induced insomnia that culminated in debilitating flu-symptoms that lingered for a number of weeks and further intensified his melancholy. Again, literature provided a lifeline.

As an employee of NYU, Tony was allowed two free courses per semester. He decided upon an English composition class and a survey of medieval and Renaissance French literature. In the latter, he was particularly taken with the figure of Clément Marot (1496–1544), who was able to successfully get out of jail on two occasions by writing long poems to Francis I. It was also around this time (February or March 1962) that Tony came across Donald M. Allen's *New American Poetry, 1945–1960* in a Village bookstore. Allen aimed to present readers to an "outsider," non-academic generation of living American poets, who were *personae non gratae* to the reigning American contemporary poetry anthology of the time, *New Poets of England and America*, edited by Robert Pack, Donald Hall, and Louis Simpson. Allen's volume represented such poets as Allen Ginsberg, Gregory Corso, Jack Kerouac, John Ashbery, Frank O'Hara, Robert Creeley, Charles Olson, Kenneth Koch, Denise Levertov, James Schuyler, and Gary Snyder—to name a few.

Allen divided his 400-page book into geographical sections, and Tony found himself most drawn to the "New York" poets (James

Schuyler, Kenneth Koch, Frank O'Hara, and John Ashbery, in particular), because he found the work more enigmatic and harder to get hold of. "I found this inspiring rather than discouraging," reminisces Tony. "I wanted to create things that were equally elusive and wonderful."

Reawakened to his own work by what he read in Allen's anthology, Tony shared some of his poems with Barbara Roberts, an NYU classmate, with whom he soon became involved romantically. He had borrowing privileges from the NYU library and had begun reading Ezra Pound and William Carlos Williams. Barbara encouraged him to read the poetry of Wallace Stevens, too, as she felt that Tony would find Stevens' sensibility appealing. After the spring semester, Barbara went off to Paris for a year at the Sorbonne, and like many people in his life during those years, disappeared.

Tony's latest living quarters were with some co-workers from the NYU Library in an apartment on East 3rd Street between Avenues B and C, which was a dangerous neighborhood then. However, it was in walking distance of NYU and the Village. In June he noticed a *New York Times* announcement for a series of six poetry readings to be held on Sundays at the New School for Social Research. He recognized the names of Marianne Moore and two from the Allen anthology. Each week he thought he might attend but didn't actually go until the fifth reading, which was Kenneth Koch's. This reading would change the course of his life.

THE NEW YORK SCHOOL

....my life is barely started, from January 1963,
when I knew it would have to be poetry or nothing.
Since then I have looked mostly like a lawyer, a broker,
but in struggles with the eternal verities,
and with always the one day to be disposed of;

at times in nostalgia for someone's past—not my own —
I told Frank that his poems made me have it for his,
and I had it for John's, Kenneth's, and Jimmy's,
and Joe's, Norman's, Larry's, Joan's, Mike's, and Jane's as
    well.
I came to know these people, but I don't really, of course,
as I go on with my work to some distant point,
with most of the feelings I had before
and the sorrow of literature I learned to keep.

—from "Addenda" (1971)

A surprise during Kenneth Koch's reading, the first one he had ever been to, was that the audience laughed often and knowledgeably. "I hadn't realized that Koch's work was quite that funny," Tony explained. "It hadn't occurred to me that poetry *could* be. I soon started laughing when everybody else did, so I wouldn't look like a fool, but I couldn't help feeling that I was the only person there who wasn't really getting it." The final of the six readings featured Frank O'Hara, who, despite not eliciting the laughter of Koch's reading, "got the same impressively appreciative ovation as Koch had the week before."

Tony started going to the Cedar Tavern more often, now that he was working at NYU, just a couple blocks away. One evening in early August, a week or so after O'Hara's New School reading, one of his Tony's roommates talked him into coming with him to the Cedar, even though Tony had not wanted to go out that evening. On entering, he recognized Frank O'Hara standing at the bar, talking to a friend (it was Edwin Denby, Tony realized later). He approached O'Hara, complimented him on his reading at the New School, and then moved on. As it happened, the only space at the bar was on the other side of O'Hara. When the latter's friend left, he turned around and said that Tony had "made his evening" by complimenting him, that he had just come from a memorial service. Then the two had a lengthy conversation, during which Tony realized that O'Hara was almost certainly gay, although he didn't seem to be coming on to him. Tony felt inadequate when O'Hara began discussing poetry, but the older poet was gracious and encouraging. When O'Hara eventually asked Tony if he wrote poetry himself, he was caught off guard and answered, "Oh, I try." O'Hara wouldn't let that pass. He persisted: "Either you do or you don't." Flustered, Tony admitted that he did. He parted O'Hara's company that night feeling excited for having met a real poet. Although the two wouldn't get to know one another until the following year, Tony felt that it might turn out to be important.

Unhappy with the NYU library job and lonely after Barbara's departure, he decided to leave New York for a time and travel to Mexico, where, through his father's side of the family, he had relatives (his great uncle had married a Mexican woman). Not being able to afford a ticket, he answered an advertisement to be one of three drivers to deliver a car to California, which entailed driving in shifts, nonstop—a chaotic trip that resulted in a three-month stay in Los Angeles. In L.A., still thinking about the readings at the New School and his conversation with O'Hara at the Cedar, he wanted to read what he could of Koch and O'Hara besides their contributions to the Allen anthology. He found *Second Avenue* (a booklet-length abstract poem by O'Hara and all that was in print at this time) challenging, but with re-reading he came to comprehend it. He was also quite taken with the "extravagant imagery and free-wheeling satire" of Koch's *Thank You and Other Poems*, published by Grove Press that year. As ephemeral as they seemed at the time, Tony's literary ambitions called him back to New York, particularly as Koch was going to be teaching a poetry workshop at the New School at the end of January. And so, with a $100 gift from his grandmother, he boarded a 72-hour, non-stop cross-country Greyhound from L.A. to New York. Halfway through the trip (which included Christmas Day), he ran out of food money, nor did he have anything to read most of the way.

Upon returning, it was only a matter of days before he found himself at the Cedar, where he encountered O'Hara again, and met Kenneth Koch:

> A day or two later, I took the train [from Rye, where his parents lived] down to the city and went to the Cedar. It certified the culture shock. The bar was brimming with the kind of assertive energy I didn't see in Los Angeles. I got a beer and made my way down the bar. There was Frank O'Hara, with a dark-haired young man. O'Hara seemed genuinely pleased to see me and introduced Frank Lima— who sized me up suspiciously. To make conversation, I mentioned that I had just gotten back from California. O'Hara said how marvelous and, naturally enough, asked me what I had been doing there. I immediately realized that the briefest description of my trip would show what an idiot I was to have taken off like that, so I fudged the details and changed the subject. I mentioned that I understood Kenneth Koch was conducting a poetry workshop at the New School and I was going to attend. "Oh, really? Kenneth is right over here." To my astonishment, and before I could ask him please not to, O'Hara walked the few feet to the bar and came back with Kenneth Koch. "This young man is going to take your class at the New School." My astonishment turned to chagrin. Koch looked at me expectantly. I didn't

know what to say. I wanted to compliment him; I had spent many hours getting to know *Thank You*, and it had been a pleasure and a revelation to do so. "Oh, Mr. Koch, I love your work. It's so … so … I was floundering for a synonym for "sophisticated," which wasn't quite right, but I knew the perfect word was there somewhere. He stood there waiting for me to finish my sentence. *Superficial* is what I heard myself saying. Koch stared at me in disbelief for a second or two, then turned away and walked back to the bar. What had I done! I was mortified beyond belief.

As it turned out, O'Hara was also offering a workshop that semester. Tony realized he had to take them both, and his mother gave him the necessary $80. Looking back, it was a momentous decision, as the two older poets had an enormous influence on his work and career. Tony was incredibly inspired by Koch's teaching style, which brought "fresh air on stale attitudes about poetry and what it should or should not be." O'Hara's manner in the classroom, on the other hand, was comparatively "low-key" and "laissez-faire," although O'Hara, unlike Koch, liked socializing after class—and anyone who wanted to could join him at the Cedar.

After one of these gatherings, toward the end of the semester, O'Hara invited Tony over to his apartment in the East Village for a drink, an invitation that Tony accepted, though not without some internal apprehension: "I thought it would surely be interesting, a privilege, even, to get to know Frank personally, but I didn't ever want to be in a position of having to fight him off." Luckily, O'Hara was gracious and read the signs perfectly: Tony was straight. O'Hara and Tony drank bourbon in the kitchen (while O'Hara's roommate and occasional lover, Joe LeSueur, after being introduced, "hibernated" in the living room and read). O'Hara, learning that Tony admired Prokofiev, as he did, put that composer's own performance of his *Third Piano Concerto* on the record player.[2] The evening turned out to be one of his more memorable in New York up to that point.

Over the next year and a half, Tony and O'Hara became good friends. Tony was soon given "phone privileges"—that is, he could call O'Hara for no particular reason, just to chat—and vice versa. There were a number of people in this category, and O'Hara's ability to have extended phone conversations was legendary. Tony told me that he had never had such long talks on the phone before or since (an hour or more was not unusual), and that they were totally involving; there was always *one more subject* to cover before hanging up.

His immersion in the poetry world grew rapidly. Shortly after the New School workshops ended, Jim Brodey, one of the poets who, like Tony, had taken both Koch's and O'Hara's classes, organized a group poetry reading at the Smolin Gallery on 57th Street for April 15th of that year (1963). He invited Koch and O'Hara, who both accepted, and three young poets (he himself making a fourth)—Tony, Frank Lima, and Allan Kaplan. This was Tony's first reading, and he recalls how he and Frank Lima devised a strategy for slowing down should either get nervous and read too fast: a kick on the leg under the table. Tony endured several of Frank's kicks as he sped his way through the allocated ten minutes, which coincided exactly with the amount of material he felt he could read in public.

Tony continued seeing Frank O'Hara socially. At the end of May of '63, Tony and Frank Lima took over O'Hara and Joe LeSueur's

---

[2] Tony was astonished to learn that O'Hara knew how to play that very concerto but had given up the piano for poetry.

apartment on the second floor of 441 East 9th Street. O'Hara stayed on another week, sleeping on the couch, until his bedroom in his and Joe's loft at 791 Broadway was finished. Tony remembers "a dorm-room party atmosphere," because on the weekend, when O'Hara got up, the first thing he would do was pop open a beer.

Tony applied to the New York City Writer's Conference, to be held at Wagner College on Staten Island in July, where Kenneth Koch would be conducting the poetry section. O'Hara convinced the conference's director, Willard Maas, to give Tony a scholarship for the $200 tuition. The twelve-day conference, in its second season, was highlighted for the poetry students by the awarding of a Gotham Book Mart Avant-Garde Poetry Prize, which had been split by Frank Lima and David Shapiro the previous year. Tony ended up being awarded the prize that summer, sharing it with Louise Santoro, a young woman in the class who had been a student at Wagner.

Over the eventful year and a half that followed, Frank O'Hara invited Tony to parties and openings, where he met such artists as Jane Freilicher, Larry Rivers, Mike Goldberg, Norman Bluhm, and Alex Katz, as well as poets such as John Ashbery, Bill Berkson, David Shapiro, Barbara Guest, Kenward Elmslie, LeRoi Jones (later Amiri Baraka), and Allen Ginsberg. He began thinking of himself as a poet and attended readings regularly. Although he never quite felt that he belonged completely, he didn't feel like he belonged anywhere else.

His work from this period lacks the autobiographical detail and flourish of the poems he would write ten years later. Many of the poems are mysterious, without coming across as obscure, and blend the real and the imaginary. In the words of Ron Padgett, "At this relatively early stage of his career, between the ages of 24 and 26, Tony Towle went beyond writing the kind of poem that is fixed in place, like a butterfly specimen, which might be beautiful but certainly is dead. Towle's poems are beautiful too, not because they form decorous displays, but because they are alive with intelligence, urbanity, and multiple voices and views, alive the way the real world is alive anytime we are brave or naïve enough to open up and let it be as astonishing as it is" (15). Take, for example, the mysterious final stanza of "Prologue":

> The pilgrims are cautious and exact
> and only a trickle comes to the edge.
> I stir slightly.
> The residue, white, is hung
> without sound.

Tony gradually began to change his style, however, beginning with "Days of Central Oil Heating," which uses some unattributed collage materials from a popular magazine. Joe Brainard moved in as a roommate in December (Frank Lima had moved out to get married). Besides scavenging materials for his collages, Joe also picked up magazines and comic books, text from which, by the spring of 1964, Tony was regularly incorporating as found sources into what he calls his "pop-collage" poems. The prime example of his use of this kind of material is a long poem he wrote that year called "Lines for the New Year." The first two stanzas read:

> The first day of January is the first day
> of the New Year. In the north
> there is snow and ice and the forest rings
> with the sound of the ax.
> So this is really a game of tag. Run across it
> as if it were a cake, and you were the knife
> cutting it right through the middle. At other times
> the clouds seem to be pillows. My target

is a cool, tax-free million. I am very calm about it.
I could end up making a good deal more.

We decided that the sun was a huge plate of gold.
We wanted to pull it down from the sky with a rope,
or across the sky, in a boat. We know how to find
the east. The east is where the sun comes up each morning.
In the morning we begin the work. There may be hundreds,
even thousands, of trees to chop down. It will be long
     after dark
before we can stop and go home to bed.

The length of the poem (523 long lines, running 14 pages in his *The History of the Invitation: New & Selected Poems* (Hanging Loose, 2001)) was composed partly in response to Frank O'Hara's challenge to keep going with it:

> I told Frank on the phone that I thought I had a perfect three-page poem. He said, "What do you mean a perfect poem? Why don't you make it longer." After a couple of such exhortations over several days, he related the story, not so well known at the time, that when he and Kenneth decided to write long poems back in 1953, I think it was, they kept each other apprised of their daily progress. Kenneth's *When the Sun Tries to Go On* ended up being about 2500 lines, while O'Hara's *Second Avenue* was a bit over 500 (and Frank's longest poem). Over the weeks, when I reported to Frank that I was up to 300 or so lines, for example, he would say, "You know, if you get to 500, it'll be as long as *Second Avenue*." By the end of 1964, I had a version that was over 800 lines, but felt the need to

cut it back over the next year or so, and have fiddled with it a little every time it has been republished.

Starting in 1965, Tony and Frank saw somewhat less of each other but continued to talk on the phone. And then, suddenly, O'Hara was on his deathbed. Tony had gone to the hospital the afternoon of July 25th (1966) with Tatyana and Maurice Grosman (by this time, Tony was working at Tatyana Grosman's print atelier on Long Island, Universal Limited Art Editions, for which position O'Hara had recommended him), but Frank had already had too many visitors and they weren't allowed to see him. Tony had the feeling that Frank was somehow "immortal" and that he would certainly recover from the accident. Tatyana Grosman wrote a personal note to be delivered to the patient. Tony's accompanying note was humorous: *Frank, we love you, get up!*—a play on the last line of Frank's famous poem about Lana Turner. When he got back home from Long Island, Irma Hurley, the actress with whom he had been living since August of the previous year, informed him that she had been telephoned by Kynaston McShine and told that Frank had died.

Frank's abrupt passing was a crushing blow to his younger, admiring friend, as it was to so many, although Tony has said that he always has a somewhat delayed reaction to tragedy. At the funeral, on July 27th at the Green River Cemetery in Springs, on the East End of Long Island (where Jackson Pollock is buried), Larry Rivers started off his eulogy with: "Frank O'Hara was my best friend. There are at least sixty people in New York who thought Frank O'Hara was their best friend." Tony considered himself one of those sixty.

Almost forty years later, Tony would encounter himself in O'Hara's *Collected Poems* (Knopf 1971) that he had read when the book was first published but which had escaped his notice. The date of the poem was July 26, 1963, and Tony knew that he had come over to Frank's loft to use his typewriter, his own having been stolen in a burglary a couple of weeks earlier. Here's how Tony describes the scene in *Memoir:*

> My recollection, aside from the fact of it being an extremely warm and humid night, is that I started working on a poem.... It came to be called "Poem of August," but I started it in July, on the 26th. I know the exact date, and that I had actually come over to O'Hara's loft to type up my previous work, through a poem of Frank's I had certainly read but never noticed the significance of until about two months ago, almost 38 years later:
>
>> you come by to type
>> your poems and write a
>> new poem instead on my
>> old typewriter while I sit
>> and read a novel about
>> a lunatic's analysis of
>> a poem by Robert Frost
>> *it is all suffocating*
>
> I had unexpectedly come across myself as an incidental portrait in the second stanza of this lovely miniature study, composed in a bittersweet minor key. In addition to my recollection of looking down at the paper in the typewriter that evening, at the large table Frank also used as a desk, I now have an additional image of myself, in profile and

from twenty feet away, Frank's perspective from the sofa near the front windows, as I sweated over my work both literally and figuratively.

O'Hara's death had a delayed but decided effect on Tony's poetic style. He believes that after he finished "Sunrise: Ode to Frank O'Hara" in 1967, the subsequent poems from that year "opened up" to incorporating his surroundings and casual thoughts, somewhat in the way that O'Hara's work sometimes did. He says that later he actually felt guilty about this, as if he had "profited" from Frank's death. He knew that the thought was irrational, but it would nonetheless pop up from time to time, until he heard Frank's voice in his head one day saying, with O'Hara's characteristic phrasing: "You'll have to take responsibility for your own work; don't blame your poems on *me*."

An early example of this newfound breeziness can be found in "For Irma During April," written a month after "Sunrise" was finished. The first few lines of the poem read:

> Now it is April, then the great bull of May,
> and then it will be my birthday and time for presents and
> the beach.
> That's when the poetry of summer descends on you
> if you are a poet, and the metaphors emit an enormous
> heat,
> tapering off to the luxuriant melancholy verse of fall.
> Then 1968 and my vote for president, and January 1969
> and 70. By
> this time my poetry improves, a compliment to the new
> administration.

Two years later, for the first time, he used the actual names of his colleagues in a poem called "April 24th," a device used frequently by O'Hara. The poem details a fictive trip to Cleveland:

> Each year our group holds a ceremony
> at the grave of some great poet, singing
> and paying tribute to his memory
> for some great poems he has left to be read and
>   remembered.
> Last spring, Edwin Denby, Kenneth Koch, John Ashbery,
> Jimmy Schuyler, Kenward Elmslie, Frank Lima,
> Bill Berkson, Joe Ceravolo, Ted Berrigan,
> Allan Kaplan, Ron Padgett, Dick Gallup,
> Peter Schjeldahl, Joe Brainard, John Giorno, Anne
>   Waldman,
> Michael Brownstein, Lewis Warsh, David Shapiro and I
> chartered a bus,
> and went to visit the Hart Crane monument in Cleveland.

The "ceremony" was also an invention. The list was a satiric riposte to those who accused the New York School of writing poems "just" to mention their friends' names; so Tony thought he would fulfill the cliché and mention them all. There is also the irony that Hart Crane, who committed suicide in 1932 by jumping off a steamship into the Gulf of Mexico, doesn't *have* a monument in Cleveland, where he grew up; but the implication is that he should.

Tony would carry these stylistic threads from the late '60s into the following decade, during which he thinks he might have written his best poems—as well as two out of his three longest ones.

THE SEVENTIES

It was deduced in my mind quite early
that I would be spending my time within its
    configurations,
and neglect somewhat
the more exhaustive aggrandizements of the body.
      —from *Swinburne: End of the Century* (1972–1973)

I met up with Tony in January 2009 to discuss the '70s. We spoke over dinner at a quiet café around the block from the Tribeca loft he shares with Diane Tyler. Tony was not in great spirits. He was agitated about health problems and was feeling lonely and overwhelmed because Diane had been away in Boca Raton, Florida, arranging for her recently deceased mother's home to be rented. He warned me a minute or two after we sat down that the '70s are even trickier to write about than the '60s—explaining, again, that his poems were separate from his life—and that it was unlikely that one could tease out reliable biography from the work. "If you take my work from '70 to '79, I don't know what a psychologist would make of it without making a mishmash of the poems and spoiling the literary effect." But as in our earlier conversations, I led in with my first question and three hours passed without a lull.

Tony met Irma Hurley late in 1964, at a party given by composer Ned Rorem. Irma was an actress admired by Frank O'Hara, who had met and seen her perform first in Ann Arbor, Michigan, when O'Hara was there for his Hopwood Award. By May 1965 Tony and Irma, who was several years older, were a serious couple, and three months later they moved into an apartment at 100 Sullivan Street and married the following year. Their daughter Rachel was born on July 12, 1967. Although Tony had some doubts about the marriage fairly early on, he enjoyed aspects of domesticity and felt a very strong connection with his daughter. He was also enjoying the fruits of his labor as a poet. All in all, it was an auspicious time of life.

At the beginning of the decade, he felt that he was part of a poetry milieu originated by John Ashbery, Frank O'Hara, Kenneth Koch, and James Schuyler in the late '50s, and that stretched into a second generation of poets, including himself, who knew O'Hara personally and were on the scene by 1965. According to Tony's taxonomy, Anne Waldman, Lewis Warsh, Larry Fagin et al. formed what was really a *third* generation, and Charles North, Paul Violi, et al., a fourth, with at least two ensuing generations coalescing by the end of the '70s. Tony characterized this "fine tuning" as idiosyncratic on his part and said that he would never try to enforce it as "gospel." Underlying the succeeding waves was a general style that connected to one or more of the four older, first-generation poets.

However the generations were defined, Tony befriended most of the younger poets as they began showing up at the Poetry Project in the years after O'Hara's death, even though they could be thought of as the "horde" mentioned in "Nearing Christmas" as the narrator jumps

> from icefloe to
> icefloe,
> a step ahead of a horde of younger practitioners,
> to whom I nevertheless occasionally turn and shout some
> advice

Bill Zavatsky, a poet and the publisher of SUN, a literary press, described Tony as something of a veteran around Saint Mark's: "When I came on the scene in the early '70s," said Zavatsky, "Tony was an established junior member of the New York School. For starters, he knew O'Hara and had a friendship with him. Also, one of his early books was published by Tibor de Nagy Gallery, which also published Ashbery and his group. That set him apart from the rest of us, in addition to his being several years older."

Tony got to know Kenneth Koch, John Ashbery, and James Schuyler better in the years after the death of O'Hara, and developed a further understanding of their poems. A thumbnail sketch of their respective contributions to his own work appears in the 1971 "Addenda":

> I know from Frank O'Hara that the poem and its setting
> are completely at your disposal,
> from Kenneth Koch that the resources of language
> are greater than oneself and thereby liberating,
> from John Ashbery that the mysterious and beautiful
> are still supremely possible,
> and supremely inspiring —
> and James Schuyler's blinding exactitude of observation,
> its serene and tremendous burden

An increasing amount of Tony's work was getting into print. He had hand-set and privately printed eighty copies of *Poems,* in 1966, and Tibor de Nagy printed three hundred copies of *After Diner We Take a Drive into the Night* two years later. Tony explained that "John Myers told Frank O'Hara that he decided that Tibor would publish me, several months after I sent him a few poems at his request—but he didn't tell me himself, he wanted me to call him, but I decided he should call me. When he didn't, I saw that it was a game, and I wasn't going to play it. Every week or so Frank would tell me that he had seen John somewhere or other and John told him that he was serious about publishing me. 'Then he can damn well tell me himself,' I would say. The very last conversation I had with Frank was on the phone a day or two before he went out to Morris Golde's on Fire Island on the trip he never came back from, and one of things he told me was that he and Norman Bluhm had run into John Myers at the Cedar, during which encounter John *again* reiterated that he wanted to publish me. Sometime after Frank died, John finally called with the 'news,' but it took him a year and a half after that to actually do it!"

One of the reasons that 1970 was a "big year" for Tony as a poet was that his first major collection, *North*, was published by Columbia University Press as the third winner of the annual Frank O'Hara Award. According to the flier from the Frank O'Hara Foundation, the award was "meant to carry on in some measure Frank O'Hara's interest in helping new poets in their work." Eligible were poets who had not yet had a book published or accepted for publication by a commercial or university press. The previous year, the judges (which included Schuyler and Ashbery) chose Michael Brownstein, which came as a real blow to Tony. "It wasn't that I didn't think Brownstein deserved it, but that, in what was an unrealistic notion of 'seniority,' I felt that I should have been the next poet to get it, after Joe [Ceravolo, who was the first year's winner]."

Tony recalls being approached by Harry Segessman, the editor at Columbia University Press in charge of the O'Hara Award series, at the Barnett Newman opening at the Knoedler Gallery in the spring of 1969, and given word in advance that the award was going to Brownstein. According to a letter written by James Schuyler to Kenneth Koch, published in 2004, Ashbery had mixed feelings about the manuscript Tony submitted: "Guess you know by now that Michael B[rownstein] is this year's O'Hara poet. John and I did a lot of buck passing to no avail since we both felt that somehow Tony [Towle] ought—or needed—to get it. But John finally confessed to finding a certain monotony in Tony's mss and that tore it."

In late 1969, Tony received an unsolicited letter from Segessman wondering why he hadn't submitted a manuscript for that year's O'Hara Award, and advising him to be sure to do so before the deadline— which was coming up soon. The fact was that Tony was put off from having been passed over in '69 and it took a follow-up phone call from Segessman to make him send a manuscript. Several weeks later, he was informed that he had won (the judges that year were Ashbery and Kenneth Koch). Tony recently had the occasion to look over the selection that he had submitted in 1969, and realized how much stronger the 1970 version was. The rejection had proved a blessing in disguise.

North, which featured cover art by Jasper Johns—the first book cover this artist had ever done—received a respectable amount of critical attention around the city. Stuart Byron, whom Tony had first met at the New York City Writers Conference, wrote a review that characterized it as "an astonishing first book," revealing "a poet of great range, precise and deft use of language, concentrated power ... it impresses as did, 10 and 15 years ago, the first books of Creeley and Ashbery, Snodgrass and Howard, Bly and Wright.... There are eight or nine poems in *North* which will be read, I feel, for a very long time" (*The Village Voice,* March 18, 1971). And for the jacket blurb, James Schuyler wrote that "a striking merit of Mr. Towle's work is the way he has found to deal with the disordered opulence of the Surrealist heritage by engaging the hermetic clarities of dreams and the associative in the life which gives rise to them and of which, he convinces us, they are an undetachable part. Poetry continues to be one of the rarest of pleasures, and those who care about it can find here a noble grace, dramatic and personal." Looking back, Tony sees the publication of *North* as his high point in terms of recognition; he had an optimistic feeling that he was at the beginning of a long, potentially distinguished career as a poet. "Things soon took a downturn," he explained wryly, "and by '75 or '76 I felt passed by altogether. Ironically, it was then that I was probably doing my best work. I mean of course recognition from the 'outside,' not necessarily the appreciation of my peers around St. Mark's."

His work of the mid-'70s was quite different from what he'd written during the time he knew O'Hara. It was less lyrical and abstract and more elegiac. And though he continued to use surrealist imagery and speech, the work was more autobiographical, albeit complicatedly so. Charles North, who is and has been an incisive and thoughtful reader and commentator on his friend's work, made an important distinction between Frank and Tony, writing, "Whereas O'Hara sometimes wrote what he called 'I do this I do that' poems, Towle's procedure is something like 'I do this, I *think* that, now I *am* that, now that has become *this*, now I'm considering what I just thought and felt about that, etc.'"

In 1975, Larry Fagin, in his Adventures in Poetry series of booklets and magazines, published a definitive selection of Tony's early (1963–64) poems, titled *Lines for the New Year*. However, the next major collection was a while in coming and was rejected by a number of commercial publishing houses. *Autobiography and Other Poems* finally came out in 1977, a joint venture of Bill Zavatsky's SUN and David Rosenberg's Coach House South. The following year, Paul Violi's Swollen Magpie Press published *Works on Paper*, a short book containing the long title poem that had particularly impressed Violi. The poet Hugh Seidman wrote a positive review of *"Autobiography"* for *The New York Times Book Review* (May 14, 1978), that concludes: "While such poetry may not suit all, Tony Towle is as skilled at it as any, and the poet here is most engaged in exploring language as a medium, aside from its strictly communicative purposes. As he says in *Autobiography*: 'Then as now my life is very / simple and of course tragic, / but my thoughts are very / complicated.'"

In 1969 Tony had been asked by Anne Waldman, the Artistic Director of the Poetry Project, to conduct a poetry workshop for the '69–'70 season (the fall of '69 and spring of '70). He maintained a fair amount of control over the conversation in class, the way Kenneth Koch had at the New School, but socialized with the students after class, in the manner of Frank O'Hara. Also, he permitted his students to give him up to six pages of poems on which he would make written comments and hand them back the following week, a procedure that both Koch and O'Hara practiced in the 1963 New School workshops that Tony had taken.

It was through these workshops that Tony, then thirty years old, met the slightly younger aspiring poets Paul Violi and Charles North. Tony immediately noticed that they had talent and, as he puts it, "were about as good as I was, or at least well on their way." They would sometimes join Tony and a number of the other students after class (there could be as many as ten) at the Orchidia, a Polish bar and pizza restaurant on Second Avenue and 9ᵗʰ Street. By the end of the evening, the bill usually ate up about twenty of Tony's thirty-five-dollar-per-session stipend from the Project. "I would almost always get stuck with the lion's share of the check," he remembers.

Tony, however, wasn't teaching for the money. He was happy to have a poetry-related activity to complement his work and family life. From 1964 until 1981 he was employed at Tatyana (Tanya) Grosman's printmaking studio, Universal Limited Art Editions (ULAE), located in West Islip, Long Island, about forty miles from New York. Tanya and her husband, Maurice, had immigrated—escaped—to the United States from Hitler's Europe in 1943. She felt the studio needed a secretary. Coming from a European background, her paradigm of a "secretary" was Rainer Maria Rilke working for sculptor Auguste Rodin. She wanted a poet, and the only American poet Grosman knew personally was Frank O'Hara, who had collaborated with Larry Rivers on ULAE's first publication, *Stones*, in 1957. Knowing that Tony was looking for a job, Frank recommended him and that got him hired.

Tony was in a unique position at ULAE. On his website he writes, "ULAE was in the forefront of the American 'print renaissance' of the '60s and '70s. Between 1957 and 1967 Mrs. Grosman invited Larry Rivers, Jasper Johns, Grace Hartigan, Robert Motherwell, Fritz Glarner, Helen Frankenthaler, Robert Rauschenberg, Lee Bontecou, Jim Dine, Barnett Newman, James Rosenquist, Marisol, and Cy Twombly to add the dimension of printmaking (lithography and etching) to their oeuvre." Tony reminisced about his duties at ULAE in an essay written for the catalogue of the 1997 exhibition held at the Corcoran Gallery in Washington, D.C., *Proof Positive: Forty Years of Contemporary American Printmaking at Universal Limited Art Editions*:

> From originally not knowing what I was supposed to do, I ended up, at one time or another, doing almost everything that needed to be done (except print or cook lunch). First, there was constant travel to and from New York on a bewildering variety of visits and errands. For many years a typical morning could begin with a hasty trip to New York as soon as I arrived and gulped down some coffee.... There were actual "secretarial" duties as well: the correspondence Tanya was expecting did materialize, billing, sending out

biographies of the artists (which had to be typed up one copy at a time) and typing a "documentative description" (artist, number of stones, paper, size, etc.) on ULAE stationery for each print that went out of the studio. Since Tanya didn't permit any erasures—which went along with her concept of perfection—this could be quite time-consuming by itself.

It was inspiring for Tony to be around important artists in their working environment, but the work took considerable time and energy away from time that he could have spent interacting with his poetry peers. The commute to work was about an hour and a half each way, and—although he worked nominally four days a week—the position entailed irregular hours and occasionally evenings and weekends. He was forced to miss literary events, which at the time he felt he really needed to go to. This made the Poetry Project workshop of '69–'70 all the more significant.

Tanya had been very supportive of Tony's poetry up through the time *North* came out, and encouraged his giving copies to collectors and museum people, as well as to the artists he had come to know through the studio. Also, she instigated and published a collaboration that paired his writing with Lee Bontecou's etchings (*Fifth Stone, Sixth Stone*, 1968), which made him one of the few writers who appeared in a ULAE *livre d'artiste*. However, by the mid-'70s her attitude began to change. Her health declined, and she had begun to think about how ULAE would continue after she was gone. "Bill Goldston, one of the printers, had taken on more and more responsibility, and was on his way to becoming the studio manager for the technical side of the business," Tony explained, "and I was supposed to take on the other aspects, which was not going to leave me time for much else. There was also a certain pressure to move to Long Island, to be closer to the studio, and I think Irma would have been all right with that, but I had the sense that my private self in general, and my poetry in particular, was going to be further impinged on. ULAE was Tanya's life but for it to become mine, I think, I would have had to pretty much give up poetry, which was Tanya's tacit expectation, but which I could not do." His full-time association with ULAE was over by the middle of 1979, though he remained involved in some of the studio's events and functions, working on a part-time basis into 1981. Tatyana Grosman died in 1982, and Bill Goldston succeeded her.

Work wasn't Tony's only source of stress during this period. His life as a husband also became more difficult through the '70s. A self-described "traditionalist," he had grown up in "the buttoned-up fifties" and basically wanted to be monogamous. On the other hand, he felt intensely pressured by the expectations of Irma at home and Tanya at work. This led to an increase in his drinking and to a number of extramarital affairs.

In 1976 Tatyana Grosman thought he needed professional help to address what was assumed to be alcoholism, and found a psychiatrist through her connections to doctors who were also art collectors. The psychiatrist, whose office was on Park Avenue, told Tony that he would give him three sessions at no cost and then payment would have to be arranged. Tony offered him three of his books in exchange for the free sessions. After the third session he decided to stop going. "I wasn't a very good patient," Tony said, "and not very forthcoming. The one thing I remember was that during the second or third session he remarked, 'You know, you have a way of talking about yourself as if you were someone else.' On my way home, I thought, *Wow, what a great perception. He's right on the money!* I even used the comment as an epigraph for a poem. I should have been concerned with being 'cured,' but instead I was caught up by what struck me as a great line. I think that says something."

Whereas he enjoyed drinking, he abstained from other drugs, as mentioned above. Tony tried marijuana on one memorable occasion but was appalled by its effect. "I remember smoking pot at a party in '64 because it was offered to me and everyone else was doing it. Bill Berkson was there, but I don't remember who else. And I quickly got seriously paranoid. I felt that everyone was hostile and 'after me,' especially Bill, whom I didn't really know very well yet. The next day, of course, I saw that my attitude had been completely skewed, and that frightened me. I didn't need paranoia in social situations. Drinking, at least up to a certain point—and I generally had a capacity that could be impressive—eliminated my self-consciousness and made me sociable and expansive. That was all the artificial stimulant I needed. And it was legal."

Though his marriage was becoming more and more difficult, and his escape through drinking and other women becoming chronic, Tony wrote more in the '70s than any other decade up to the present. Life was hectic and turbulent and entirely without the predictable rhythms many writers need to produce quality work. Somehow, though, he kept at it. The inspiration was there, and he always seemed to be working on something. From the poems of this period, he feels especially positive about "Nearing Christmas," which he considers a breakthrough. It also chronicles a line "from" Frank O'Hara—a line he heard in his head but in Frank's voice, complete with Frank's inimitable inflection, while composing the poem, and he included it, which is Frank saying: "You call that lyric you big bag of shit?"

The poem opens with some "gratuitous" lines and then references the fact that Frank O'Hara's *Collected Poems* had recently been published. The poet (who is in his apartment on Sullivan Street) then talks about having a "quick drink" before going to Bloomingdale's to look for Christmas presents. But he keeps writing and drinking (Bloody Marys) and *not* actually going. A sub-plot in the poem is that Tony, like everyone else that Frank knew, is astonished by how many wonderful poems Frank had written that nobody knew about. The final lines of "Nearing Christmas" read:

> Finally I have gone to Bloomingdale's
> and I am back.
> You call that lyric you big bag of shit?
> I am not talking to myself,
> or in that manner to a great poet of the past,
> that must be Frank, talking to me;
> I am at last fully awake in this mortal life,
> for the few years in the middle,
> and I keep myself opaque and I don't regret it,
> on the promontory.
>
> Frank you've got to help me
>
> and there is an answer but not at this moment.

In a move that he characterizes as "inexcusable" and even "insane," Tony left Irma in 1979. Rachel was twelve years old at the time. Although he hadn't wanted to repeat the messy 1960 debacle with Monica and their infant son Scott, it nevertheless happened again. He felt that the relationship with Irma was beyond repair and impossible to continue. He realizes in retrospect that by 1979 he was vulnerable to meeting one woman (rather than running around) with whom he had a rapport, whose affections he could escape to. The woman turned out to be Jean Holabird, an attractive painter who provided the trigger and seemed to be the answer. Tony and Jean would live together in her Tribeca loft on Warren Street for the next fourteen years. Rachel finished middle and high school and then attended Bard College. Tony did not see his daughter again until 1985, and not regularly until 1998. Rachel moved to Los Angeles for a time, before returning home in 2008 to help care for her mother, who, in addition to dementia, suffered from an array of health problems. Tony helped Irma during her final months, until her death in September 2009 at the age of eighty.[3]

"OLD AGE"

> Well, like the Mets I'm coming up to bat in the bottom
> of the 9th, or the 8th, if I'm lucky,
> but far behind in the game —
> and the music seems to have stopped to listen.
>
> —from "Digression, 5/10/03" (2003)

I met Tony at our regular Tribeca café in late May 2009 for our fifth conversation, which was supposed to cover roughly the previous decade. He showed up looking fresh, but complained of feeling gloomy and seemed cranky. His health hadn't been good, and the idea of turning seventy the following a month wasn't making him feeling any better:

> Seventy is a big number. It's a medieval concept that I
> guess is taken from the Bible: three score and ten, and then

---

[3] Irma worked in market research until the mid-90's, and then for an art-postcard shop in SoHo. Over the years she also participated in acting workshops and occasionally gave a performance. She continued to live in the Sullivan Street apartment for the rest of her life.

it's the beginning of old age. I think whatever years you get after 70 are gravy. I know the present-day American positive attitude is that you're never *old*, which is largely a strategy of the medical establishment to keep older patients from being depressed; it has nothing to do with how Americans who are under, say, 50, really feel about old people. I'd like to tell the next 40-something doctor when he says I'm young if he'd mind me going out with his theoretical 30-year-old unmarried sister. After all, she and I are both young, so what would be the problem? Or, how would he feel about switching ages with me. Prefer not to? Why not? So everybody's *young* forever, until one day you die of old age. The underlying concept behind all this is that *there's something wrong with being old*. Of course my complaining about this kind of conventional wisdom the way I'm doing *is* young—it's adolescent!

Tony surmised that part of his unhappiness had to do with the fact he hadn't written anything in over a year. This was especially disconcerting because Tony had always considered poetry his only consistent life thread—"through the various relationships, getting and losing jobs, and not having money or not quite enough or very little, poetry is the only constant, and I've had a very difficult time writing in the last year. I stopped writing for a while when I got the proofs back for *Winter Journey*. So I took a "vacation," and when it was time to get back on the horse I'd forgotten how to ride."[4]

---

[4] From shortly after we spoke into 2010, there were a number of successful new poems, including one written in commemoration of his seventieth birthday. However, he then went another two and a half years without being able to finish anything. Tony reported that the writer's block finally ended late in 2013.

Physically, although he had good days and good stretches of days, his mobility and overall health had been on a gradual decline since the early days of the millennium. In 2005, while vacationing with Diane and her elderly mother, he started convulsing in a taxi on the way to a hotel in Vienna, and then again in the room, which required a house call from a doctor. This inexplicable illness went away in a couple of days—Tony refers to it as "the Habsburg virus"—but it was jarring. Most frightening of all, he experienced what's often called a "mini-stroke," known as a transient ischemic attack (TIA), the following year, as Diane and he were preparing to leave the city and travel to Olivebridge, about 110 miles northwest of the city, where Diane owns a modest home:

> We were getting ready to go upstate in a rented car, and I didn't feel well; I didn't know why. I had gotten enough sleep and I hadn't even had anything to drink the night before. But for some reason I didn't feel well. And I got up from my chair and fell over into some boxes. I dragged myself back to my chair, my desk chair, and just sat on it, and Diane came out from her room and my speech was slurred. So she called an ambulance right away. God! Had that happened an hour later I would have been going 75 on the New York State Thruway and I wouldn't be talking to you now!

After three days in St. Vincent's Hospital and a battery of inconclusive tests, Tony was released and put on blood pressure medication. In 2008 a new primary care physician diagnosed atrial fibrillation, which probably caused the TIA. At around the same time, he had an episode of diverticulitis, but fortunately did not need an operation. In the five years since his hospital stay, his various health conditions have either plateaued or have worsened in proportion to his advancing age. As a preventative measure, Tony has tried physical therapy and Pilates, both of which have helped.

Money has been his most persistent source of stress. After leaving ULAE, Tony spent four years working as an administrative assistant to the founder of the Center for Entrepreneurial Management (CEM), in SoHo, beginning in 1982. Compared to ULAE, the work was easy but uninspiring, and he recalls starting to take lunch breaks at 2:30 at Fanelli's, a bar he and Jean frequented. He worked at CEM for over three and a half years, and in fact got Jean a job there too. However, around Christmas 1985, "I pointed out to the boss his contradiction in the company policy on holidays, and was summarily relieved of my duties."

After six months on unemployment benefits, Steve Mariotti, whom Tony had met at CEM, looked Tony up at Fanelli's. He wanted to start a nonprofit company to teach at-risk young people how to start their own businesses, and he needed someone to write his letters, help write lesson plans, and work on other, essential written materials. The company would be called the National Foundation for Teaching Entrepreneurship (now the Network for Teaching Entrepreneurship), and it turned out to be a twenty-eight year relationship. Tony is the co-author of a series of books on how to start and operate a small business, which he finds ironic given his checkered employment and financial history. He stopped working for the company in 2010, although he continued to help Mariotti with his personal writing until April of 2014.

Health and financial concerns aside, he feels lucky to be in a stable relationship with Diane. The romantic part of his life had been spotty since he and Jean Holabird parted ways.[5] The time leading up to their

---

[5] Tony chose not to say much about the break-up during our conversations.

dramatic (melodramatic, really) break-up was long and unpleasant. Jean started having an open affair, and Tony had an illicit one with a woman from the neighborhood, which he managed to keep secret, in spite of the fact that he has remarked that "Tribeca had all the privacy of a medieval hamlet."

Tony had moved out of the Warren Street loft in January 1994, and took over his brother's minuscule studio apartment on East 29th Street. It was the first time he had lived above Houston Street, and the first time he had lived alone, in twenty-eight years. The relationship with the woman in Tribeca ended after a year and a half. "So now I'm alone again at the beginning of '95," Tony explained, "and I didn't like it. And I'm getting older. I'm in my mid-fifties. All the bars on Third Avenue are full of young people. When I walked in, I didn't exist. It was too depressing to sit there by myself." Once or twice a week he'd take a cab down to Tribeca and have a few drinks in bars "where everybody knew me," although there were precious few opportunities for romance in his old neighborhood.

It was at this point (September 1995) that he decided to put a personal ad in the *New York Press,* a paper that had an extensive personals section. "And when you did that back then it was a big decision; and it felt big—not quite shameful, but sort of pathetic. It's like, you have to do *that* to get a *date*?" He was lucky and met a charming woman whom he saw for a little more than a year. However, she broke off the relationship in December (1996) by leaving a message on his answering machine when he wasn't home.

"It was devastating," said Tony. "I didn't see it coming. And it happened two days before a reading at St. Mark's, which is always an event for me, and four days before we were going to go upstate to Billy and Diane Collins' annual Christmas party and then spend the night with Paul and Ann [Violi] in Putnam Valley." Her decision was influenced by the fact that she was a serious Christian (Presbyterian), even though she had a sense of humor about it. Tony was seriously secular.

A bartender friend at Puffy's, from which Diane lived two doors away, introduced her to Tony the following year. She was working through a messy divorce and was literally pushing herself to be social and talk to people. Initially, she'd get a drink and then sit outside Puffy's on a bench, so she wouldn't have to talk to anyone, before going back up to her loft. Gradually, she found the courage to have her drink at the bar. The two spoke in February, met again in September, and in November became romantically involved. Tony says that Diane saved his emotional life. *A History of the Invitation: New & Selected Poems 1963–2000,* is dedicated to her with a phrase in Italian that refers to Dante's book-length homage to Beatrice: *for Diane/per la vita nuova ("for the new life").*

Tony has also been grateful for the company and humor of his closest colleagues. Although they became friends thirteen years earlier, it wasn't until 1984 that Tony began meeting Charles and Paul regularly, once a week—at Fanelli's—for an hour of "talking shop" and gossip. This tradition was carried on at a succession of Village coffee houses and soon included Bob Hershon as a regular, with occasional appearances by Larry Fagin, Ted Greenwald, and others. The last such get-together was in December 2010, with Tony, Charles, Paul, and Bob. In January, 2011, Paul confided to Tony and Charles that he had been diagnosed with cancer. He died that April. Much of Tony's (and Charles') time and energy after Paul's death was dedicated to the planning of memorial services and organizing his selected poems.[6]

---

[6] *Paul Violi's Selected Poems 1970–2007* was published in September of 2014 by Rebel Arts, an imprint of Gingko Press (Berkeley, CA).

Also, Tony spent a good deal of time organizing his archival papers in 2011, and they were sold to Yale's Beinecke Library in 2012.

WORK

A lyrical poet with a taste for the surreal, Tony Towle has spent his career recording an imagistic and sensorial autobiography that seamlessly blends the disparate elements of his life into an unmistakable voice. The "Towle" persona is alternatively bombastic, wistful, erudite, and sardonic. Although the work has been compared to O'Hara's "I do this, I do that" poems (see quote from Charles North, above), it also possesses Whitman's "multitudes," as well as a fascination with New York City. The places, personalities, and cultural vernaculars of New York saturate the poems, which have the fast-paced feel of city traffic: images, perspectives, and tones shifting like street scenery from the backseat of a yellow cab. And behind it all, a frenzy of dynamic emotions propels each piece. Reading across Tony's extensive *Selected Poems* (2001), one encounters the portrait of a man searching for the still center of a turning world. At the heart of this search is a deep yearning for spiritual wholeness reminiscent of Wordsworth or Keats.

Perhaps because of the intensely personal nature of his quest, Tony's work by the early '70s took a turn away from the more abstract quality of his earlier published work. Narrative poems like "The Morgan Library" and "Nearing Christmas" present the reader with a concordance of experiences unified by the familiar cadences of his narrative style. Each of these poems presents a slightly different version of Tony, culling a discordant constellation of scenes, sequences, thoughts, associations, and dreams. Whether historically accurate or fictional, these snapshots from a life create an effect that is more traditionally autobiographical than many of his fellow New York School writers. There are poems about eating a hamburger ("New York"), walking to the Morgan Library ("The Morgan Library"), Christmas shopping somewhat drunk in Bloomingdale's ("Nearing Christmas"), or visiting a new Korean laundry in the neighborhood ("Ethnicity"). And poems like "Recapitulation" and "(April)" move fluidly back and forth across the border between wakefulness and dreaming, often blurring the boundaries between the two.

Despite this bewildering diversity of experience, the poet-speaker maintains a meticulous personal chronology. Tony's poems are carefully dated, as are many of the events described in them. The long poem *Autobiography* (1970–73), for example, is showered with temporal markers—e.g., wheeling his daughter Rachel through Washington Square Park in 1970, a moment in 1950 (when he was eleven years old) standing "in the playground next to my school," and several fleeting memories of Queens Boulevard and Rego Park from the "late forties." Here are other examples from the poem:

> Long before 1950 I knew that one of the numerous years
> would bring death, as 1939 brought life,
> in the way that two poems on universal themes
> open and close an important collection...

> *

> I walk into the wind, continually,
> have lunch on velvet burgundy tablecloths with friends,
> dress for dinner in elegant striped jackets,
> or fabulous gray suits,
> a pestilent green hat or short furry slippers,
> fashion with charm like the perennial space that it is
> always pulling at your leg,
> or concocting a simple soup. I enter another year, 1973...

His interest in chronology goes beyond a lifelong fascination with history. Objectively speaking, Tony's life didn't follow a predictable course; nor was it particularly easy. In addition to his struggles with marriage and fatherhood, he lost his mother to cancer relatively early; was separated from his brother and two sisters, who were put into foster care; and had a strained relationship with his father, who was unequipped to raise a family after his wife's death. Tony's twenties were marked by personal upheavals and uncertainties. After leaving his first wife and infant son behind in Washington, D.C., he struggled with borderline poverty as a young man in New York City. The practice of writing helped him to piece together a narrative sense of self that was threatened by disruptions and setbacks. No matter how helter-skelter life may have seemed, though, poetry enabled him to infuse his existence with temporal continuity, as evidenced in later poems like "In the Coffee House" (2001):

> I told Diane I'd be here 'til six. Waiting
> for a girlfriend *literally* is a great improvement
> over the afternoons at the Figaro;
> and in fact it's cool to *have* a girlfriend at my age
> I think amusedly to myself
> behind the overpriced coffee,
> 2.95 to contemplate the traffic
> fleeing down the avenue and into the past
> which has brought me up to the present,
> where I put down my pen, figuratively.

A meticulous attention to chronology can also be found across Tony's 100-page *Memoir:*

I had begun, surreptitiously, writing poems in 1960, in Washington, in reaction to and escape from a two-and-a-half-year-long teenage marriage that had become unendurable (14).

Sometime in 1961, after finding Carol was no longer a factor, I had started going to the Cedar Bar.... (36)

It was sometime in May that I fell in love (61).

Even though it would be another five years—only after I had a book published—before I would answer the question "What do you do?" with "I'm a poet"—it was *then*, as 1963 drew to a close, that I knew it was so (99).

It's not surprising then that Tony's perennial gloominess is especially pronounced during periods when he isn't writing, or isn't writing particularly well. In his own words, "through the relationships, the bad relationships, jobs, losing jobs, and not having money, or very little, poetry has been the only constant thread." This thread has played an important psychological role for Tony. A significant amount of research has been done in narrative psychology on the need for individuals to construct and maintain relatively coherent personal life stories. Without a degree of narrative coherence, one's ability to process life-disrupting experiences can break down, and ego integrity can fall into jeopardy of breaking apart altogether. Judging from Tony's work, it's likely that the flexibility of verse offered him such coherence.

The social nature of many of Tony's poems also helped him to be in the world, allowing him to cultivate a thicker social ecology than may have actually been present. Tony lived alone intermittently after leaving his parents household as a teenager. Other than his daughter, Rachel, and girlfriend, Diane, his most long-lasting social relationships have been with his poet and artist friends and colleagues. There are many, many names scattered through his work, including Charles North, Paul Violi, Larry Rivers, Robert Motherwell, Frank Lima, Ted Berrigan, David Shapiro, John Ashbery, Kenneth Koch, James Schuyler, and, perhaps most importantly, Frank O'Hara. These connections were cemented through the Cedar Tavern and Saint Mark's Church, in addition to the years he spent at ULAE. To this day, despite health limitations, he sometimes attends the readings, dinners, and book launches of his writer friends. But as he put it ironically but ruefully in a poem composed for his seventieth birthday, "there are many more things I could drink to / than my capacity these days can support...."

Some of his more social poems contain conversations that he probably couldn't easily have had in life. The depth and intimacy of these exchanges are uncharacteristic of Tony's social persona and code of masculinity. Either the material is too personal—such as in "A Note to Charles North"—or else the person in question is no longer living—such as in "Nearing Christmas" or "Thoughts at Frank O'Hara's *City Poet* Party, 6/9/93." In the absence of a traditional nuclear family unit (at least not a consistent one), poetry helped Tony to foster a different kind of family—a community of fellow writers with whom to share, celebrate, and commiserate. For example, the poem "July 6th," written in 1983 after the death of Ted Berrigan, signals an attempt to bridge a chasm between himself and a poet with whom he was never particularly close:

> And there is the soft thump of insects
> on sandy skin, while I absorb the news,
> two days after Ted Berrigan dies

and the sky seems to sag
and open up a space, the one in which
we didn't really know each other,
though for twenty long years,
which are suddenly shorter.
At this point a painter
could reach down
for a little cerulean blue
to cover the hole in the sky
while I search out a caption for the scroll below.

The image of the painter conjures a hope that artists can cover over loss and estrangement with bright, life-affirming colors. In a similar way, poetry engenders an ethos of intimacy between friends whose personalities prohibit heart-on-sleeve confessions. The poem "A Note to Charles North" provides a prime example of this. "It's approaching death of course, if you want to know, /" Tony writes, "and I don't think you want to know, / which makes two of us, at least…." The poet/speaker is reluctant to share the mortal terror that has overcome him, so confesses it in a "note" addressed to his friend. The fact that the poem is rather longwinded and abstract, despite being called a note, infuses the confession with a buffer of humor. In Freud's view, humor was a mechanism through which painful, threatening and/or socially unorthodox thoughts were expressed. Or consider the final lines of "Nearing Christmas"—elegiacally addressed to Frank O'Hara:

You call that lyric you big bag of shit?
I am not talking to myself,
or in that manner to a great poet of the past,
that must be Frank, talking to me;
I am at last fully awake in this mortal life,

for the few years in the middle,
and I keep myself opaque and I don't regret it,
on the promontory.

Frank you've got to help me

and there is an answer but not at this moment.

The only person on the planet capable of offering him the type of help he needs most is no longer living, "a great poet of the past." Likewise, in the 1993 poem "Thoughts at Frank O'Hara's *City Poet* Party, 6/9/93," Tony unsuccessfully attempts small talk at a book launch for Brad Gooch's biography of Frank O'Hara, *City Poet*. His voice in this poem is as humorously self-effacing as it is anguished. The long-dead O'Hara speaks directly to Tony at the end of the poem, as he does in "Nearing Christmas." Frank tells Tony that he can no longer help him in the ways that he once did when he was alive:

> "Don't be truculent, you're not young enough anymore —
> in fact you're thirteen years *older* than I am now, so act it.
>   There's
> John Ashbery, go over and say Hello. It's thirty years later
> and I'm *still* getting you invited to parties, but this
> is the *last time*. As Siegfried said to Brünnhilde on the
>   way up to Valhalla,
> You're on your own for the rest of this saga, baby,
> *I'm* going to get a *drink*!"

Yet again, O'Hara and his wit barnstorm to the rescue! Frank gives Tony a tough-love pep talk (that Tony of course has invented) while Tony wanders around a gathering of New York School artists who knew him when he was young and new on the scene. Despite the fact that he spent decades affiliating himself with this particular group of artists, he fears that no one ultimately cares about him. To make matters worse, everyone present is claiming Frank as his or her own. O'Hara's reference to Siegfried and Brünnhilde refers to the lovers in the final opera of Wagner's *The Ring of the Nibelung*. Siegfried leaves Brünnhilde behind for an adventure on which he is killed, breaking her heart. Judging from this reference, O'Hara was much more than a poetic mentor; he was the encouraging father figure that Tony never had. Again, it's in a poem that Tony reaches out, filling interpersonal distance with lyrical intimacy.

From a literary perspective, however, all of this is tertiary at best. There's a lot more to say about Tony's poetry than claims about cohesive identity and sociality. His poems are propelled by a desire for something perpetually out of reach. This yearning is evident from Tony's earliest published work. Take the closing stanza of his 1963 poem "Prologue:"

> The pilgrims are cautious and exact
> and only a trickle comes to the edge.
> I stir slightly.
> The residue, white, is hung
> without sound.

Many of his poems feature mythological and historical figures on difficult life journeys, often in pursuit of something quasi-mystical. Examples include Gauguin, Orpheus, and the mysterious pilgrims cited above. The whiteness, in this case, suggests a space perpetually beyond us, an eternity that is both exhilarating and terrifying. It's the whiteness of the margin into which Emily Dickinson's dashes point, or the ego-dissolving "oceanic" that Freud theorized about in *Civilization and Its Discontents*. Even though Tony would be chary of referring to this whiteness as mystical, it is. According to the twentieth-century Christian theologian Paul Tillich, to be religious in a modern sense entails holding something beyond the finitude of the self as one's ultimate concern. A self-described agnostic, Tony doesn't use religious lingo to characterize his search, but the impulse behind it is for nothing other than the infinite.

A sustained note of mystery is also struck in my personal favorite from Tony's early New York poems, "Today." The language haunts me as deeply now as it did years ago when I first read it. A surrealistic quality marked by shifts in voice and enigmatic disjunctions make the poem hard to grasp, at least semantically. Emotionally, though, it's hauntingly familiar. The affecting final lines read:

> Today the phantoms pass through rock.
> The phantoms move higher in the rock, the smoke,
> the fumes, and the powdered ash.
> Instinctively I scale a tree, I vanish.
> The clouds are torn apart to show the moon;
> he drops to a bench; the telephone rings,
> a hypnotic background for the words.

There is an abundance of movement upward—e.g., the scaling of a tree, phantoms moving up through rock, the quickening of instincts. The poet/speaker vanishes, and then returns two lines later in the third person singular, as if the "scaling" culminated in a momentary escape from subjectivity. One can't help but to think of T.S. Eliot in the box circle of *Burnt Norton*, or John Ashbery's more numinous interludes.

The poet/speaker of a Towle poem will move through a crumbling city propelled by desire, often lonely or overwhelmed, but intent upon attaining a redemptive apogee, whether it's the consummation of carnal desire, the cool sudden flash of Platonic truth, or the illumination of self-knowledge. A poem that comes to mind immediately is "The Morgan Library" (1970), which begins:

> Up, gracing the void with intellect, I noticed a ring,
> encircled by rows of shimmering diamonds,
> walking, feeling prosperous and losing weight,
> to the Morgan Library. For young people there was a pin,
> expressing love in simple cascades of diamonds,
> on 34th Street
> which we give no relief walking and walking,
> looking for something to stick it into,
> women and children first, apples, walnuts, melons,
> the calm transparency of plastic, the grudging
> response of lead, or the rolling fog or even a jar of
> > worms!

The sexual act of penetration within these lines moves from the possible to the improbable to the absurd. But far from being funny, the imagery is laden with desperation and sadness. The poet/speaker, now no longer one of the young, has nowhere to put his desire. Like a hungry ghost, his encounter with the void brings him to the incomparable Morgan Library. There he sees the fragile manuscripts of Keats and Shelley and proceeds to feel as if he, too, is trapped under metaphorical glass and desirous of erotic, geographical and spiritual freedoms:

> At times I would like to go to a foreign country
> and forget myself and America;
> American women are complicated and beautiful,
> and their soft arms cling in loving silence,

but at times I feel there are other women
who wait for me in vain.

Tony's poems are especially powerful when the romantic vision
that impels his search for the sublime falls short. Desires go unmet,
and he is forced to deal with the inconsequential. The pathos implicit
in such cosmic letdown is palpable enough to evoke tears. A poem
that fits this description is "A Note to Charles North," quoted from
earlier. This three-page poem, composed in January 1973, was writ-
ten to thank Charles for having come out late on Christmas Eve in
1972 to help him. Charles was settling in for the night with Paula,
having just gotten his young daughter to sleep, when Tony phoned
drunk and depressed from a bar, prompting Charles to put on his
coat and travel downtown to help his friend. The second stanza goes:

> It's approaching death of course, if you want to know,
> and I don't think you want to know,
> which makes two of us, at least,
> lying like rugs, under threat of economic difficulty
> and caught in the threads of a major civilization,
> but a stone's throw from the perimeter, a new
> world for the stone, the upper half of him,
> parted by the city's colored street, the city's terrace
> where roses bloom so many times, in reminder,
> in spades, of the spring that destroys me.
> Thank you, by the way,
> brooding on the darkest ruins in time imaginable,
> another eve of Christmas and too much smoke,
> from the hearth and from the far zone
> which to reserve me for itself for later
> preserved me.

Here there is no shortage of existential disappointment. The grieving plain of his life is strewn with debris, literal and figurative. He is depressed by the holidays, by his approaching death, by economic difficulty, and by "the spring that destroys me." But the smoke from the far zone, which promises to consume him down the line, simultaneously preserves him, leaving him on the promontory to write his poems as if his life depended on it, which it did, and does. It was through the act of writing that Tony was able to make aesthetic (if not emotional and psychological) sense of the obstacles that fell across his path. As he puts it wryly in "Nearing Christmas:"

> no event in your life is of the slightest importance,
> but there is nothing you cannot use;
> the unceasing events of your boring life
> occur only for the success of a particular poem
> awaiting your efforts on the horizon.

PAUL VIOLI

APPROACHING URANUS

Will everyone have a front row seat
Do our eyes appear as headlights
Does the glow increase while we think
Explain these nipples on my chest
Where was the Land of Cockaigne
What about the face of Charlemagne
Why warts
Did someone discover the wheel by stepping
on his fingers at the brink of a hill
Can you appreciate the modulations of a vicious belch
Where are the plays of Menander
Does the Loch Ness Monster ring a bell
Do impure souls lend color to the flames
Do you find these myths entertaining
Or superfluous
Am I a Calvinist
Whither Martin Bormann
Has someone already asked you these questions
Have I already asked you these questions
How will I know you're not lying
How will you know you're not lying
Is perfection comforting
What if it isn't

INDEX

WET BREAD AND ROASTED PEARLS

Through a filmstrip of train windows,
I watch the river coast by, mist
climb the Palisades to open sky.

Hudson line. Gravel trackbed
dusted with snow, bank rock and piling
blackened with oil, barges
half-rotted on granite slabs
where a deer dips her head in bent reeds

and then steps out onto shore ice:
One long wave of white ice
nightwinds caught at its farthest reach
between arrival and return
and held gleaming above the tide.

The ideogram for "recognition,"
you know, was formed from the figure
of a deer: to leap from a standstill.
And when the thin ice
suddenly collapses
and I see the doe slide, stagger,

but somehow remain on a wobbling piece
that carries her
out into the mist—there's
the ideogram for "amazement":
to be standing in that splendor.

Blue cliffs lean against bluer sky,
blue as the wreaths
around smokers' heads,
sleepers' heads, readers' heads;
blue as the blurred tattoo on his arm,
the old man in the next seat:
the tall ship faded into his skin.

Once across the city line
riverbank turns to rubble.
Row after row of mounds,
a ransacked graveyard
of mistakes buried under broken images,
brick, busted block, scrap metal,
crumpled sheet-rock, tires,
charred planks, sand piles
dumped on lots
glittering with crushed glass.

Of the numerous ideograms
for "To fill in the blanks"
one is based on a recognizable figure
heaving gigantic hourglasses
off a train just before it bursts
under a roaring city
and stalls.

Another contains
a figure, someone who abhors
crossword puzzles, someone

like me, newspaper
in hand, stultified
by a maze of blanks.

Eighty-nine down: More lavish clues.

One across: To be reasonably
suspicious of zeros and words
that contain too many o's.

Two across: Prosopopoeia.

Fifty-five down: Monotonous.

Three across: Puzzle is to Mystery
as Grapefruit is to...

Five across: Rhymes with orange.

Eight across: Of Aquitane, as in:

Thirteen across: Of summertime, as in:

I think I'll throw away a poem, take
a nap and then go stand in the sun.
Or lie beside you on the dock awhile
and write another one.

Or wait for you to open your eyes
and figure out
what this little kid on the beach
is all about.

He's pulverized pearls with a rock
after he popped them
like corn in a fire,
a handful of fake pearls
he cast on the water
along with some bread for
Thirty-four down: Type of fish,
a.k.a. "pumpkin seeds."

Crumbs and pearl dust—sunnies
rise out of the murk
like stupidity approaching speech,
then veer off
without a nibble, without a blink.

And, like Twenty-one across:
A magician
who somehow tricks himself,
makes his own charms
disappear and finds himself
empty-handed in the unyielding air,
the kid just stands there
staring at a puddle of oil
that floats between dock and raft,
its slack colors slipping away

PAUL VIOLI

like The Lost Planet, turning
with every move this one ever made.
And whatever made it move:

Gases change to moiling seas,
squashed continent to coastline.
Greenery fades to saltflat
and back again.
Empire and ignorance,
each with its course, its color
—a different color for every age,
every eon, migration and flood,
dust and flood, famine
and soaked plunder, flight
and pursuit, white and yellow
and blue, the aerial swirl of snow
and disease, peace
and convulsion, belief and denial.
And there it goes, sight out of mind,
leaving me

to watch you finally wake
and wonder what dreamt you into being;
to almost know it, but to lose
that, too, in shadow and water,
and then watch reappear
another circling fly, another
horsefly and gnat, dragonflies

and, Twenty-one down:

PAUL VIOLI   229

The "wizardry in daylight"
that allows them to stay,
suspended
in the ever-expanding sky
that sweeps back
to Thirteen down: Bombay,
where one afternoon, leaving
that city on a slow, quiet train,
trackbed raised
above flooded fields,
no land in sight,
I could see nothing
but sky mirrored in water
and the tremendous sun drawing
its hourlong reflection
across horizonless blue.

Two perfect circles, swirling,
identical,
slid into one, hung there,
where an early world
that greeted the advent of yellow
with flutes and bells
and pure geometry,
intersects Thirty-four across:

The Grapefruit,
the one you thought I'd aimed at you
just because it punctured the wall
next to your ear.

The glaring, almost magical fact of it,
a grapefruit stuck in sheetrock.

One warm afternoon, hillside
yellow with fallen leaves, starlings
began to flock, as plentiful
as the leaves still left in the maples.
All that clatter, so many,
thrown every which way
in the shrapnel wind,
people stepped warily out their door
and wondered what was going on.

Even we, who had seen it before,
could only raise our arms
and laugh at what was as much
a feeling as a sight,
a sound, the sky-blown praise,
the mayhem, the soft yellow ground

now as blank as Eight down,
the winter you decided
to freeze me out, kept
the house as cold as a morgue.

Days I didn't hear
you speak except in your sleep,
so that one morning I woke
to the sound of your voice
and a cold draft

and the noisy sparrows
at the window.
I lay there cold and tired
listening to Five down: The first sign
of spring, cheap-talk
in the dismal, breaking light.

And when the smoke alarm,
its battery worn down,
began to beep, the signal
at first indistinguishable
from the birdcalls
but then growing louder,
triumphantly monotonous
in their absence, I remained
Three down:
A man of my word.
And that word is
Fifty-five across: Disingenuous.

For the rest of that week
above Peekskill Hollow Road
the ridge loomed, fledged with treetops
rising row behind row.
By the next, the colors
had flown, and for days
in that gray intricacy
of italics and twigs,
the slightest sound reached
a distant, whispered edge: pencil

PAUL VIOLI

scraping paper, dry leaves
blown over pavement; a vine
rubbing stone; a piece
of cellophane flying out of nowhere
on that remote lake, skidding
after me as I skated.
And suddenly, as if I were
the figure on the cover
of Two down: A novel
of grim pursuit, regret
and Gothic dread,

there was, inexplicably,
more cellophane,
scraps of clarity, a swarm
of blanks and withered smiles
whirling around me
before I simply turned
and headed back into the wind,
scraping a few more edge songs
out of what stays, what goes...

what happens when we
find ourselves in Eighty-nine across:
An Important Event
in the History of Punctuation:

We lie in the dark and listen.
The window open
you wait for me to guess

what you already know:
that voice so lovely and strange
you can't believe
I don't remember what it is.
And then I do:

Miles of lake ice shift and thaw,
singing the changes
that move as lightly as years
and the lifelong questioning
that keeps turning me toward you
and One down: The origin
of the question mark

in darkness and the curve and line
of your spine, your neck
your chin, your ears, your
legs and breasts and my open hands
—Hands, rough, calloused,
sliding over your taut silk
they sound like breath.

ON AN ACURA INTEGRA

Please think of this as not merely a piece
Of writing that anyone would fully
Appreciate, but as plain and simple
Words that attempt to arouse whatever
Appetencies you, especially, depend
Upon language to fulfill; that drench you
In several levels of meaning at once,
Rendering my presence superfluous.
In other words, welcome this as a poem,
Not merely a missive I've slowly composed
And tucked under your windshield wiper
So that these onlookers who saw me bash
In your fender will think I'm jotting down
The usual information and go away.

APPEAL TO THE GRAMMARIANS

We, the naturally hopeful,
Need a simple sign
For the myriad ways we're capsized.
We who love precise language
Need a finer way to convey
Disappointment and perplexity.
For speechlessness and all its inflections,
For up-ended expectations,
For every time we're ambushed
By trivial or stupefying irony,
For pure incredulity, we need
The inverted exclamation point.
For the dropped smile, the limp handshake,
For whoever has just unwrapped a dumb gift
Or taken the first sip of a flat beer,
Or felt love or pond ice
Give way underfoot, we deserve it.
We need it for the air pocket, the scratch shot,
The child whose ball doesn't bounce back,
The flat tire at journey's outset,
The odyssey that ends up in Weehawken.
But mainly because I need it—here and now
As I sit outside the Caffe Reggio
Staring at my espresso and cannoli
After this middle-aged couple
Came strolling by and he suddenly
Veered and sneezed all over my table
And she said to him, "See, that's why
I don't like to eat outside."

AS I WAS TELLING DAVID AND ALEXANDRA KELLEY

My brother swears this is true.
And others have willingly
—generously testified,
As they did that other time when
After leaving an office party
They pulled off the expressway,
Walked into a place he'd never
Been to before, and ordered
A few more drinks while he
Headed for the lavatory.
But as he was crossing the dining room
On the other side of the bar
This vicious fight broke out.
Two women—well-dressed, tall,
Gorgeous—tore into each other,
Punching, clawing, swinging
Spike-heeled shoes, pulling
Each other's hair, and my brother,
Aghast, jumped between them
To break it up, grabbed them roughly,
Held them apart, berated
Them, tried to shake some sense
Into—when he gradually pieced
It all together: the changed look
On their faces, the disapproval,
The utter silence of condemnation

That everyone aimed not at the women
But at him, the fact that
It was a supper club theatre
And he had just jumped into
The climactic scene of a play—
But this, I hasten to add, is not
About my brother but his neighbor,
A man whose roof needed repair;
A man who, more than most, feared heights.
A ladder to this neighbor
Didn't ordinarily suggest the kind
Of elevating work that joins
The material to the spiritual,
So before mounting it he called
His children over and, as he wrapped
A rope thick enough to moor a barge
Around his waist and lashed
The other end around the car bumper,
Carefully explained to them
How they should steady the ladder
Until he had climbed onto the roof.
Up he went, not overstepping
But securing both feet on the same rung
Before proceeding to the next:
A trembling man on a trembling ladder.
He squirmed over the drain,
Crawled up the not very steep slope,
Flopped over the peak, then slid
Inch by inch down the rear slope
Until he felt confident enough

To kneel instead of crawl,
To sigh and take a deep breath
Before he began to cut a shingle.
Perhaps the first horripilating signal
Was a subtle tug on the rope,
Like an angel plucking a harp string.
Perhaps it was a sudden tautness
Around his waist, or, perhaps,
He heard the station wagon door
Slam shut, then the ignition,
The engine roar to life, or
Slowly grindingly churn before it
Kicked in and he was yanked heavenward
Then jerked back, slammed, twisted,
Keelhauled belly up, belly down,
Over the roof, dashed onto the driveway
To be dragged, dribbled,
Bounced hard along the road, his
Wife looking this way and that
As she drove on, wondering
Wherever were those screams coming from?
Doctors, police, all believed
She could very well have not seen
The rope; could not, with windows
Rolled up, have ascertained,
While they lasted, the source,
Proximity and intensity of the screams.
And I, for one, though respectful
Of the family's desire for privacy,
Think for numerous, inevitable,

Irresistible philosophical,
Sociological but mostly religious
Reasons, this place, this event,
This man deserves a shrine
Which, if donations are forthcoming,
I am willing to oversee
The construction of
At 145 Sampson Avenue,
Islip, Long Island, New York.
That's right, that's the name
Of the place: Islip. I swear.

WRITTEN IN A TIME OF WORRY AND WOE

I stopped and leaned over the footbridge rail.
Far below, roaring by the library,
The stream plunged through deep winter with force
That follows a spring thaw, re-enacting
In a short stretch its ever-varied course.
I watched it flow clear under clear black ice,
Churn frothy under gray, tunnel and swirl
Under snow, pool and spill, then slide over
And under overturned stumps and debris.
I watched until I thought: February—
The apex of the year, and felt so far
Above the sum of whatever I've known
Or seen or done that I couldn't care less
What I must have lost to feel so cold and free.

From FURTHER I.D.'S

I

I was the first to write in that willful
And various style the Greeks had no name for.
Perseus considered my enemies victims
And said that I broke my jaw-tooth on them.
My friend Horace said I grind out
Indistinguishable poems
And called them bratverse.
He complained I wrote so much
My funeral pyre would need
No other fuel than my own books.
To hell with his pesky notions of perfection:
As some sages sing
It's the impurities that give color to the flames.
Of one of my poems only one word
Remains: Vulture.
Though little survives of the others
But phrases and flotsam, I am as I was,
Loving crowds and solitude, with the shoreline
My sometime refuge from them and myself,
Wind at my back, sand as fine
As powder, as wispy as smoke
Blown across the glowing hardpack,
Big-eyed skittish creatures, oddities,
Little beauties and what-not
Shadowed by scavengers,

The chance a surprise or two
Will ignite an idle hour.

Who am I?

II

Plato and Aristotle argued over this and that,
Over something from nothing,
And over what made me laugh.
In childhood I retreated to a garden shed
Where I wrote and studied so devotedly
My indulgent, gentle father, to remind me
Of neglected chores, tied an ox to my door.
Three days passed before I noticed the beast.
To prevent another beast, money,
From distracting me, I gave most of mine
To charity then squandered the rest.
I went to Athens but told no one there my name,
Not even Aristotle, for why should I have
A little renown bestowed on me
From merely visiting a famous place?
Better to have my visit give a place
Something to brag about.
I titled my first book *The Little World*
And right before I died at 109
Published my last, *The Great World*.
Plato wished to burn every copy he could find.
Nothing exists but atoms and empty space;
All the rest is rumor and guesswork.
(Poetry is worthless.)

Meanwhile, entangled, awhirl or dancing freely
In the vastness of such a hive, try to remain fearless.
Aristotle said my laugh was an echo
Of the highest ethical good: Cheerfulness.
But Seneca thought it contemptuous, citing reports
That I would laugh at strangers in the street,
And the fact that, Abdera being my hometown,
A nasty cackle was called Abderian Laughter.
Couldn't they hear it all together, a chorus of one?
Kindly mirth, empathy, reckless sympathy, scorn,
All in the same raw ardent voice,
Cockerel or rooster—young or ancient,
Ancient and eager in the dawn.

Who am I?

III

Three explanations circulated amongst the people
As to why on the opening night of my play
The theater roof collapsed:
I. The rafters were rotten.
II. The gods had passed judgment on a bad play.
III. The gods were jealous of its greatness.
Though obviously the best, the third
Explanation was not entirely correct.
I waited until speculation peaked
Before pronouncing the real reason:
The gods knew a finer play
Would never be performed there
And thus deemed the theatre obsolete.

I was popular.

I improved the lot of the poor.

I was accused of killing my mother.

I had a big belly and skinny legs.

To restore morale after Rome burned

I invited thousands to a party in my private gardens.

All feasted on my generosity, all admitted

To being overawed by my musical compositions,

And all agreed that the torchlight—torches

I myself designed, each one containing

A bundled living Christian—made the night

As bright as daytime in August.

Who am I?

IV

I built this house so the stairway expands

As it rises above the sea, not to a front door

But directly to the roof: rectangular, red,

Flat to its rail-less edge, a runway

Below the infinite night where on occasion

I like to dance with extremes balanced

In my outstretched arms, in my open hands.

Critics describe my writing as surreal.

After the Eastern Front, Surrealism was child's play.

I wrote a novel—sad, wry, horrible, subtle, brutal—

That was a string of vignettes, portraits

Of desperate cosmopolites and grim commoners,

An elegant necklace slowly tightened into a garrote.

Soldiers whose eyelids had frozen and broken off,

They don't mean to be rude,
Forever staring back at the reader.
When Naples was liberated, the doors
Of the asylum thrown open, the lunatics
Ran joyously through the streets, down to the bay,
And then, like Europe, didn't know what to do,
And stared at each other in a wild despair.
The Tatars thought of war as the dead killing the living
And to savor that irony liked to tie a prisoner
To a corpse that would rot and slowly kill him.
When the Finns trapped a Russian army,
Surrounding it in a forest with a ring of fire,
Herds of terrified horses leapt out of the flames
Only to land in the river the minute a 30-below wind
Arrived and froze it and them immediately.
They're still there months later, mile
After mile, horseheads protruding through the ice,
Necks stretched back toward the charred shore,
Horseheads about the height of a bar stool
On which I sit and smoke and talk to you.
A mishandled corkscrew and from one of my cold
Numb fingers a drop of blood seems to have fallen
Into a glass of white wine … or ice water.
It dissolves in undulant swirls and disappears.
I wonder how far I can follow where
The invisible dancer behind those veils is leading me.
On my deathbed, perplexing a few witnesses,
I embraced Catholicism and Mao's communism.

Who am I?

V

I introduced Swinburne to cognac.
He told me the Goncourt brothers dropped by
Unannounced one day to find him in his study
Reciting Aeschylus in the original
To a severed hand he held before him.
He kept it for that sole purpose, enticing his muse,
In a jar of formaldehyde on his desk.
They fled without saying a word.
Attacked on a beach in Somalia, I fled,
Swimming with a spear through my face
Back to the ship where my rescuers
Hauled me aboard by the shaft.
From time to time I drank to excess.
Mint-juleps, Brandy-smashes, Whiskeys,
Gin-slings, Cock-tail sherry, Cobblers,
Rum-salads, Streaks of Lightning,
Morning Glories: I drank myself through America.
Many found my respect for Mormonism
As disagreeable as my admiration for Islam.
I mastered 29 languages,
Each increasing the force of the cascade
Under which I held my crystal glass.
Soldier, spy, explorer, anthropologist,
Historian, pilgrim, poet, sexologist:
Because of my service to the Crown
I expected a diplomatic post.
My antagonists saw to it that I was sent
To the Bight of Benin, a miasmic,

Fever-ridden deathtrap where I found
It easy to despise all races equally.
One king crucified a fellow in honor of my visit.
I almost went mad and begged to be recalled.
In my three years there I wrote only nine books.
When I died my wife, my dear, darling Isabelle,
That glorious auburn-haired woman, burned
My diaries, journals, papers, though she resisted
Consigning to the flames one work of erotica
Until my ghost commanded her to do so,
And then only on its third appearance.

Who am I?

VI

I preached to large congregations.
I published theological treatises.
Scripture was always on my lips
But those who did business with me
Soon found I was a mere swindler.
At length I turned my attention from
Theology to the worst part of politics.
I belonged to that class whose office it is
To render in troubled times to exasperated parties
Those services from which honest men
Shrink in dusgust and prudent men
In fear, the class of fanatical knaves.
Violent, malignant, heedless of truth,
Insensible to shame, insatiable of notoriety,
Delighting in intrigue, in tumult,

In mischief for its own sake, I toiled
For years in the darkest mines of faction.
I lived among libelers and false witnesses.
I was the keeper of a secret purse from which agents
Too vile to be acknowledged received hire,
And the director of a secret press whence pamphlets,
Bearing no name, were daily issued.
In this way of life, I assumed more names
Than the devil himself, and at one time
Flitted among four different lodgings
In the malebolge of London.
When my conspiracies were detected
And my associates were in dismay,
I laughed and bid them farewell,
And told them they were novices,
That I had been used to flight,
Concealment and disguise, and that I
Should never leave off plotting while I lived.

Who am I?

VII

I do not see very well in the dark.
I have a bald red head.
I like to sunbathe,
And while I do I defecate on my feet
To keep them cool and clean.
I am attracted to rubber and plastic
Which I like to rip off your house and car.
If you bother me I will hiss at you,
If you threaten, I will vomit on you.

Caveat Lector: I can with stunning accuracy
Spew a good ten feet.
My Latin name, *Cathartes Aura*,
Means cleansing breeze.

Who am I?

VIII

Why was I known as the King of Peace?
I was a tightwad.
I mired my court in squalor while pouring money
Into my prize accomplishment: a brigade of giants.
My ragtag, penurious diplomats
Scoured Europe for recruits.
My ambassador to London received a bounty
Of 1300 pounds sterling
For finding a 7' Irishman.
I gazed upon that brigade like a boy
Cherishing his collection of toy soldiers.
Since I would never risk them harm in battle,
I, of course, avoided wars.
Atheists, Catholics, Calvinists, Philosophers:
They were all the same to me: laughable.
I lived under a cloud of tobacco smoke
And malevolent rage.
If I met a lady on the street, I'd give her
A good kick and send her home to her brats.
If I met a clergyman, I'd cane him.
I loved Swedish beer, hunted wild boar
And slaughtered partridge by the thousands.

I despised literature.

I don't know whom I detested more,

My daughter or my insolent, Francophile son.

He asked too many questions.

I woke him up each morning with a canon blast.

I threw dinner plates at him

And forced him to eat putrid food.

I broke his flute over his head.

I tried to strangle him with a curtain cord

And dumped him in a dungeon.

He grew up to become a military genius

But was accused of depravity

And perversion so abhorrent

They would make a satirist blanch.

Who am I?

Answer Key

I	Lucilius
II	Democritus
III	Nero Claudius Caesar Augustus Germanicus
IV	Curzio Malaparte
V	Sir Richard Burton
VI	Robert Ferguson
VII	Lappet-Faced Vulture
VIII	Frederick William I

NOW I'LL NEVER BE ABLE TO FINISH THAT POEM TO BOB

Now I'll never be able to finish that poem to Bob
that takes off of a poem by Bob
where he's looking out the Print Center window
at a man in a chicken suit
handing out flyers on Houston Street.
Mine has Plato saying man is a featherless biped
and Aristophanes slamming a plucked chicken
on the table and declaring the definition apt but flawed
and it ends with Francis Bacon
dedicated empiricist
experimenting with frozen food
stopping his carriage in a snowstorm
and hopping out to stuff a chicken with snow.
It worked but Bacon got pneumonia and died.
Without making a pun on bringing home the bacon
the poem closes on Bob saving Bacon's life
with chicken soup. It would have been a long poem
and it would have made a lot of sense
and shown why I believe Bob Hershon is a wise man.

LIFE

PHOTOGRAPH BY DAVID KELLEY, 1992

Paul Violi (1944–2011) was sixty years old when we first met at the Fish Bar in lower Manhattan. He was 5'8", handsome, good-natured, and had graying dark hair. Physically robust, he had the hands, shoulders, and chest of a workingman, which granted him an aging virility that was absent in many of his poet friends. Paul was a heavy cigarette smoker and enjoyed socializing after teaching his classes at Columbia, NYU, and the New School University. He enjoyed sharing absurdist anecdotes about everyday experiences and did so with the impeccable timing of a good comedian. Depending on whom you were asking, his frenetic lifestyle of adjunct teaching, late night socializing, and high speed racing up and down the Taconic Parkway between Putnam Valley, New York, and New York City was either a marvel or a source of serious concern. Despite his gregariousness, he was a private person and had the reputation among friends as someone who preferred dealing with setbacks quietly and stoically. Over the course of five sprawling interviews conducted at the kitchen table of my apartment on the Upper West Side, Paul had me in stitches hearing about how his family's Christmas rental, a large house in West Palm Beach, Florida, was infested with fleas, which devoured everyone but him; or how the publisher Lita Hornick loyally continued to employ a printer even though he was going blind until one book (written by poet Janine Pommy Vega) was accidentally printed in blue ink; or how he was once in a car crash with his wife and kids on his way to a holiday party that resulted in his being splattered with sauce from a pasta dish his wife, Ann, had prepared, which led witnesses to think when he stepped out of the car that his injuries were far worse than they were; or how his wife was bitten by a snake two summers earlier, minutes after they had finished listening to an audio recording of Book IX of Paradise Lost. *He died of aggressive pancreatic cancer one year after I defended my dissertation, and eight years after our first meeting. When I initially approached Paul in 2008 with my proposal, he agreed to the project with a characteristically self-effacing joke: "I don't know whether to think along the lines of Stein's* Three Lives *or Moe, Larry and Curly. No, seriously, it all sounds wonderful. And as far as interviews and times go, you can count on all my help."*

EARLY HISTORY

Yesterday also has its leaves, newspapers
blown down the bare avenues
and streets of yet another city
entering the wide morning behind you, surprising
you that this light, often unnoticeable breeze
which constantly blows in your face,
which carries sights through your eyes
like leaves through air,
can move these cities farther away
than islands driven by an ocean stream...

—from "Harmatan" (1976)

Paul Randolph Violi was born on July 20, 1944, in New York City. The Violi family soon moved to Greenlawn, Long Island, shortly after the Allies defeated Japan. Paul was the middle child, with an older brother and younger sister, with whom he kept in regular touch. His mother and father were born into first-generation Italian immigrant households in Brooklyn. They met young, around the age of ten, and a family legend has it that Paul's father ingratiated himself by throwing either a snowball or tomato at his bride-to-be and hitting her on the caboose. His father came from a family of fifteen that valued the arts, in addition to pasta dinners with lots of talking and red wine. One uncle was a prodigy on the piano and another received a Master's in comparative literature from Columbia University. Opera and jazz, notably Caruso and Ella Fitzgerald, were frequently played on the phonograph at night and on Sundays.

On the rural North Shore of Long Island, Mr. Violi co-owned and managed Russwood Drugs and, in time, two other drugstores. Paul and his siblings were put to work at the age of ten, stocking shelves and helping with inventory, and later working behind the lunch counter. Paul describes his father as supportive, loving, determined, sensible, genial, and easy-going. He never really got mad, rarely consumed alcohol, and—aside from one memory of his having said *"There's the son of a bitch!"* in response to seeing his former captain in the Navy appear on one of Edward R. Murrow's televised interviews—Paul can't remember his father ever cursing. A World War II navy veteran stationed in the South Pacific, he was quiet about his war experiences until his seventies, when he started opening up more. Paul gained a sense of who his father was as a young man when he read his wartimes dairies after his death in 1995. He learned, for example, that his father had taken a long train trip to see the western United States after being drafted at the age of twenty-four. He also read about his father's experiences on a PC 173-foot submarine chaser amid the threat of typhoons and "suicide bombers," and the intensity of seeing Tokyo in ruins after the incendiary bombings ordered under the command of Colonel Curtis Lemay, a.k.a. "bombs away Lemay."

Paul characterizes his mother, who was suffering from dementia during the time of our interviews, as supportive, though nervous. She was "a pretty feisty lady," he explained, "with two sisters with whom she was *very* close. She was full of vitality, very loving, and determined." Both parents were encouraging of his early interest in poetry and made sure to supply him with anthologies of verse, which he read with great interest from his early teens on. They also placed a good deal of emphasis on education by sending their eldest son, Peter, and then the following year, Paul himself, to The Stony Brook School, an Episcopal day and boarding school located in Stony Brook, not far from Huntington, New York. Paul describes its "preppy" demographics as comprising 200 students, including "two Catholics, one

Jew, two blacks, and one girl." Morning chapel was mandatory and the boys were required to wear gray slacks, a blazer, and a blue and white striped tie.

After his sophomore year, Paul felt bored and intellectually restless and no longer wanted to attend Stony Brook. At the time, a cousin was going to an all-boys Catholic school in Mount Vernon run by Marist Brothers called Mount Saint Michael's. His cousin liked it there, so a decision was made to enroll Paul as well. He attended for his junior and senior years, boarding during the week and taking the train home to Greenlawn on weekends, where he enjoyed "hunting, trapping, and having fun." Paul describes himself as having been "very wild" during high school, but in a way that generally avoided parental detection. Part of this had to do with the fact that Mount Saint Michael's was closed for saints' days, which meant that Paul was free to roam around the city with friends on days and nights when his parents thought he was in school. "My father wasn't religious and my mother went to church on Sundays," adding with smile, "not every day some saint was being celebrated."

When I asked him to recount a memorable episode from his days at Mount Saint Michael's, Paul told of being smashed across the face by a history teacher named Brother Charles Patrick after a morning assembly on first day of class. Brother Patrick asked Paul to stay behind as the other boys filed out for class. Paul remembers sitting as Brother Patrick made his way up the bleachers—and then cracked him across the face with an open hand on the grounds that he was talking during the assembly. Humiliated and stinging with pain, Paul spent a moment deciding whether or not he should shove the man backward down the steep bleachers to the gym floor. Instead he took his punishment quietly, though vowed to himself that he would wait for the right moment to retaliate. An opportunity arose at the annual student/faculty football game a few weeks later. "I tried to hit him every play," Paul explained. "And eventually I put him out of the game. He couldn't raise his arms."

Paul loved sports, whether football, wrestling, baseball or track and field (shot-put, discus and javelin). He also did a fair amount of dating from an early age. Ann, however, was his first love, and Paul vividly recalled seeing her for the first time. He was in a boat with friends in Northport Harbor on the North Shore and watched as a pretty young girl swam from the shore to the boat and surfaced in a bikini. Her face appeared through the water next to the boat and he remembers thinking that she was the most beautiful girl he had ever seen. Ann was from nearby Centerport, New York. He had a number of girlfriends through his teenage years, but there was something special about Ann, something he had a hard time forgetting when they were separated. Like Dante's Beatrice or Petrarch's Laura, she is the muse in many of Paul's poems, especially ones written during his twenties and thirties. Take the opening lines of an erotic poem, "Centerport, N.Y.," from *Automatic Transmissions* (1970), which was the first pamphlet that he ever published:

> her clothes slid off
> with the ease that makes smoke rise
>
> and we waded in   gradually
>
> two thoughts entering a consciousness
>
> dove and came up
>
>   shining

and laughing as the water laughed

> against her belly.

COLLEGE, PEACE CORPS, AND JOURNEY EAST

We are undertaking a voyage
to an ancient island
separated from the continent
by more than water and dialect,
boasting on its own heritage
and rules of governance.

—from "Brochure" (1981)

Paul studied English and Art History at Boston University from 1962 to 1966. He was not always a serious student and read what he wanted to read. Some of the coursework, however, interested him quite a bit. In particular, he recalled influential upper-level genre classes: one on satire, one on Renaissance Literature, and another on Wordsworth and Coleridge. The great satirists—mainly Pope, Swift, Dryden, Voltaire, Rabelais, Byron—played a hugely formative role in his literary sensibilities, in addition to the Romantic and Victorian poets and contemporary novelists like Amis, Donleavy, and Heller. When he wasn't reading books, a good deal of his time was spent exploring Boston, hanging out with his friends and dating a series of women. Boston's Back Bay "was a great place to be single and to have your own apartment," he said with an evocative grin.

When it came to meeting other poets he had far less success. "The poets whom I met there, who were deliberately making themselves known as poets, I didn't like much. They struck me as pretentious. And also, at that time I was writing stuff that … well … it was good that I didn't publish it. It was dull, actually." Much of Paul's early work was influenced by the Imagist poetry of Ezra Pound, which derived its technique from that poet's idiosyncratic reading of classical Chinese and Japanese poetry that stressed precision, clarity, and economy of language, while forgoing conventional rhyme and meter. Paul's next poetic stage (after graduating college) involved writing cryptic symbolist poems that were largely inaccessible to anyone but him. Paul purposefully destroyed virtually all of this work in late '67—either thrown away or willfully lost. This was the same year that he moved back to New York. After college, he spent a little less than a year as a Peace Corps volunteer in Nigeria and then an additional year travelling across Europe and Asia until he reached Nepal.

The Peace Corps required that after graduation he go to California for training, immediately followed by seven months as a surveyor and mapmaker in Nigeria (from December 1966 until June 1967). Shortly after landing in Lagos, a number of his fellow volunteers, when they encountered the heavy humidity and saw that the walls in the airport were riddled with bullet holes, literally turned around and went home. Paul, on the other hand, had no desire to return—he was seeking adventure, much as he had as a child and much as he would continue to do through his life. In the six months that followed, he completed maps and surveyed land for the Nigerian government; camped and hiked; rode motorbikes into remote villages that seldom encountered white people; was attacked by various wildlife; dealt with dengue fever and dysentery; and encountered tribes on the brink of a bloody civil war. Seven years later, in 1976, he published a book-length poem in forty-nine sections that chronicled his Nigerian experiences. Called *Harmatan*, the book is Paul's most transparently autobiographical. A period review characterized it as "accomplished as most of Violi's work, but contains little of the language distortions, tv-generation wit, or structural fireworks of his other poems. It is instead an almost prosy, straightforward series of impressions: the impressions of a poet distanced from events in order to report them as objectively as possible."

The narrative voice in *Harmatan* is set in the second person singular. When I asked about this decision, Paul said: "I was talking to a different person in a different place, and given the abrupt transitions of the time, both seemed remote. It's a poem about memory, and each section is organized around a different place and the rest of the section clusters around it. To borrow from a well-known metaphor of Ezra Pound's, it was like putting down a bunch of metal filings on a piece of paper and then placing a magnet underneath and then they all shoot together and form the pattern of a rose. So, each one of those sections is just what popped up, coalesced, fell into place. I would remember a place and then other memories would cluster around that place. I wanted a poem based on plain language and direct observation." Section five, for instance, begins with the line "Kaduna's tin roofs glistening in the afternoon." This line is immediately followed by an associated memory-cluster:

> Peanut sacks piled into hundred-foot pyramids.
> Groups of lepers and beggars
> converging on customers outside of stores.
> Streets thick with exhaust fumes.
> Khandee's heavy breasts.
> Cock-eyed and hipless. Flowery skirt.
> Keeping mosquitoes off you all night.
> Sweet, stoned, perpetually drowsy.
> Black leg next to a white leg in candle light.
> Tongue leading a cool breeze over your skin.

[5]

Many of the sections contain funny vignettes and images:

> Another invitation from the emir
> to come over for a few beers
> at ten in the morning.
>
> [11]

Or:

> Free sales demonstration.
> Made it himself out of spare parts.
> Muzzle-loading pistol
> the length of a sawn-off shotgun.
> How can he tell how much powder
> to use when he's pouring it in the dark?
>
> [34]

But just as quickly, the images gather into a darker human portrait of superstition, prostitution, extreme poverty, the effects of malnutrition on children, and the haunting aftermath of tribal warfare:

> Staved-in doors. Ransacked rooms.
> And on the other end of Kano, right outside
> the old city's wall's eroded embrasures:
> mass, unmarked graves
> and past them, more fields, mud compounds,
> bundles of firewood, children with bad teeth...
>
> [31]

As is characteristic of much of Paul's work, a redemptive premium is placed on the absurd and strange, neither of which was lacking for a young American who hadn't traveled beyond the United States:

An oven made by packing mud
around discarded fuel drums.
A tongue for breakfast.
Unsliced, lying in the tin bowl
as if it had just pronounced its last syllable.

[17]

Also in the montage are moments of arresting beauty and wisdom:

Fine dust above the goat paths
suspended in the sunlight
then drifting upward
as if the ground were raining on the sky.

[48]

A cloud looks snagged on a tree.
Spring water flows off like excess clarity.
In the village, the women never stop
to take a breath, but sing
with the ease of a stream,
of the earth ceaselessly emptying itself.

[49]

Feeling the buildup to a civil war, later known as the Nigerian-Biafran War, Paul hastily abandoned his Peace Corps assignment and attempted to cross the Sahara but was denied entrance into Algeria. So he made his way, alone, to Côte d'Ivoire, where he met a young woman with whom he travelled to Paris. After a brief romance, she continued on to Ireland to visit friends, and he to Italy. Paul described his progress eastward as follows: "Then I thought I would go to

Greece. It wasn't so far away. And then I figured I'd go to Turkey, and once in Turkey I thought Iran is just down the road, so I went to Iran … and that's how I ended up in Nepal eventually…. I think of it all as an accumulative blur. But it was a lot of fun; it was very interesting; being an American at that time was a blessing because it was such an admired country throughout the world, despite the escalating war in Vietnam."

In a twist of fate, Ann, who was also in the Peace Corps, happened to be in Turkey while Paul was travelling through the country. But he didn't learn she was there until after his return. A poem in his book *Splurge* (1982) called "Anatolia" reflects upon the Turkish winter with a consciousness of her presence:

> Snow falling on the desert, snow falling on the sea, wake
> up in between, wind filtered through bullet-ridden stop
> signs, taste the cold spoon of dawn, the crazy birds are
>   jump-
> ing in their nests, your hair is my black moon, your lips
>   touch
> my ears, breathe the sound of beautiful new cars speeding
> past me as I drive through Turkey again, only this time I
> know you're there too, though don't know exactly
>   where…

Other poems contain images from his journey east. Examples include "Scrounge" in *In Baltic Circles* (1973), about India, and also a moment in the long poem "Wet Bread and Roasted Pearls" that recalls a striking visual memory from his time in Mumbai:

> where one afternoon, leaving
> that city on a slow, quiet train,

trackbed raised
above flooded fields,
no land in sight,
I could see nothing
but sky mirrored in water
and the tremendous sun drawing
its hour-long reflection
across horizonless blue.

When I asked if his year travelling was the highlight of his life, he grinned and then said that it was the highlight of that time in his life but that there have been many since.

RETURN TO AMERICA

Before Americans' color preference
For most major appliances
Changes from Avocado to Harvest Gold,
You will have learned to seek harmony and trust.
—from "Dry Spells" (1982)

Paul recalls feeling let down upon returning to the United States. Much of this had to do with where the country was in regard to Vietnam in 1967; also, he felt a growing disenchantment with what was called "the consumer society" or "conspicuous consumption" at the expense of American values. His return was colored by an acute awareness of social injustice: "I went from places where sick and starving children were ubiquitous and then came back to America and worked on a cruise ship and the contrast gave me whiplash. Also, I was very politically involved at the time in response to what was going on in the world. I mean LBJ and Vietnam—and I thought the war was all a total sham—no justification as to why I should kill Vietnamese. It didn't make any sense to me. I'm not sure it was as transparently a sham as the Iraq War, but I felt just as strongly. Congress didn't declare this war, and it violated every sense I had of politics and the American Constitution."

Although he attended antiwar demonstrations, his experience of becoming politically active was mixed at best. While he opposed American foreign policy, he was simultaneously critical of "the radical left," which, in his words, "[tried] to manipulate legitimate protest to a more extreme action, or an extreme end, which is just to blast the whole thing apart ... and I resented seeing the way they tried to do that... They took a Constitutional right to speak up and took it to a place that reminded me of the Bolshevik provocateurs...."

Luckily he was never drafted and recounted his elation upon being declared 4F at his draft board interview in the early summer of '68. Going into the interview was jarring because he had been working as a clam digger on Long Island. He was tan and in good condition physically, just the kind of specimen that the army was looking to send to the frontlines. He changed into a button-down shirt on the way to the interview and buttoned it to the wrists and neck. Furthermore, he devised a strategy of showing a lack of interest in anything political. He figured that the government was looking for any attitude that was strongly held, the psychology being that someone who vehemently opposed the war could as easily channel that intensity into killing Vietnamese. In addition to his apathy, having contracted Dengue fever and an extreme case of dysentery while abroad, and a purposefully low score on the intelligence test, disqualified him from the draft. Upon hearing the verdict of 4F, he left the federal office building and did a series of cartwheels in the parking lot before climbing into his girlfriend's Mustang convertible and speeding away into a beautiful summer afternoon.

Others of course were not so lucky. Two friends from Boston University were drafted and came back psychologically damaged, drug addicted, and/or alcoholic. One of the two wrote Paul and Ann regularly letters that were incoherent and at times painful to read. Although the PTSD was overwhelming, Paul pointed out that his friend's sense of humor hadn't been entirely destroyed. Decades later, the friend came upon a Holiday Inn "Tudor Room" restaurant that was being demolished and took several large portraits of sixteenth century aristocrats. He then proceeded to send three of the portraits, 2x3 feet in size, to Paul and Ann as postcards by writing their address on the back and placing several hundred stamps at the top right corner.

It amazed Paul that some returned from Vietnam relatively unscarred, whereas others were reduced to lives of pathos and dysfunction. Paul discussed the second of the two veteran friends in an interview he did that was published in *Pataphysics* magazine in the nineties. In it, he recounts attending a David Letterman taping when the friend came to New York City for a visit:

> I was with a friend I hadn't seen in a while, and I was dismayed by the way he looked. He was still a young man but Vietnam and booze had turned him into a frail, trembling old man who had to use a cane. He had tickets to the show, and I thought that was an odd thing to do. He had a pal with him, a big guy who was on crutches, and they had been drinking quite a bit. When we entered the studio the perky minions who seat the audience took one look at us and panicked. We didn't fit their demographic.

They didn't want us anywhere near a camera angle. I think we were wearing black raincoats. I naturally insisted that we sit in the front row; they wanted us in the back row. We compromised and they seated us in the second-to-last row—in a corner! *[Laughter]*

MARRIAGE AND NEW YORK CITY

And I like the sweet, weary feeling
of going sleepless, aimless through city streets,
have the action and ebullient tones
carry me like the first wave-borne beer can
to near a pristine shore....

—from "One for the Monk of Montaudon" (1981)

After working as a clam digger and being declared 4F, Paul moved to Manhattan and reconnected with Ann. The two were married on June 29, 1969, and lived for a while in an affordable apartment Paul found on the Lower East Side. Wanting to make inroads into the downtown poetry scene, Paul began spending time around Saint Mark's. As mentioned, The Project offered Monday and Wednesday readings, much as today, and poetry workshops on other days, several of which Paul took. Although the majority of his classmates were ambivalent about the material he was writing (not to mention its sheer quantity), he felt encouraged by his workshop leaders. Tony Towle, who Paul thought was the most talented poet around the place, ran the most valuable workshop of all. His initial impression of Tony was of a man who knew art, music, and literature inside and out and who was very much involved with contemporary New York poets and artists.

Tony was magnanimous in the attention he gave to Paul's work and willing to share his connections, getting Paul and Charles North, who was also in the workshop, invited to a number of literary gatherings. "It seemed like the three of us were just naturally compatible friends, in terms of humor, our take on poetry," Paul explained. "We became friends very quickly. There were a lot of after-reading and after-workshop get-togethers at bars. We were interested in literature—you know, not just the poetry scene. And our humor—our senses of humor—complemented one another's. We had a lot of fun, and I also learned a great deal from them."

Paul found himself writing more than ever, and publishing too, although with a "mindless prolixity" he'd later regret. Some of this work found its way into his first pamphlet, *Automatic Transmissions*, which came out in 1970. It was a work that he'd express ambivalence toward later on. I emailed Paul to ask why it wasn't listed on his author website, to which he responded:

> Good question about *Automatic Transmissions*: good in the sense that I never clearly decided why I left it out, just knew I didn't want to include it for a number of reasons and had and still have mixed feelings about it: (A) I felt that some or all of it had been subsumed by the later book, *In Baltic Circles*, therefore making it superfluous. (B) I had outgrown it, didn't care much for it, and pretended it never happened. (C) I disliked the cover and still do. (D) Pamphlets are supposed to be ephemeral, except the ones I still like and have elevated them to the rank of book. (E) Sometimes I read it and think I should list it.

The pamphlet was published by a small press Paul co-founded called Swollen Magpie Press, after a line from Ezra Pound's *Pisan*

Cantos in which the poet refers to himself as "a swollen magpie in a fitful sun." At the time of its publication, Paul and Ann were spending the summer in New Hampshire where Paul was working a construction job. In the evenings they would hang out with a group of young men and women in the area, one of whom was an artist and volunteered to do the cover. Paul agreed without ever seeing a sample of the artist's work. The cover consists of a rather unconnected grouping of black line drawings, including the hood of a car, an old woman's face, a young seductive girl kneeling, and a small classical-looking building behind a well-dressed man.

Regardless of how the cover looked, there was hardly any time to worry about it. Things were happening, and there was a great deal of excitement in the air. New York life was a whirlwind of aesthetic energy and social happenings, the nexus of which was Saint Mark's Church and the Poetry Project housed there, where Paul taught workshops and was briefly interim director, as well as serving for years on the Advisory Board. The Poetry Project of that day was full of colorful personalities and lots of interesting, albeit erratically organized, workshops and reading series. Paul met lots of new people and packed his days with readings, art shows, and get-togethers. He enjoyed long nights of socializing with other poets and artists affiliated with the downtown scene. He was introduced to the paintings of Rivers, Oldenburg, Dine, and later Grooms, all of whom he felt were able to create beautiful things "in quite original ways."

Also influential was a postmodern architectural turn that came about in urban centers in the late-'60s and early-'70s, namely the work of Robert Venturi. Architecture caused Paul to think and feel in ways that began to affect his writing. He put it like this in a conversation with me: "What appealed to me was the freedom, the openness, the allusive playfulness with which they drew on the past to counteract the cold and brutal severity—*you know*—all that concrete and [those] sharp angles. What mattered was not a clean wholesale break with the past, but a continuing homage to or conversation with [the] poetry I loved." He began writing a lot of new work and various people in the New York City art world began to notice. On May 11, 1972, out of the blue, Paul received a letter from someone named Lita Hornick. Lita was the head of the Kulchur Foundation and publisher of Kulchur Books. She and her husband, Morty, were wealthy art collectors and patrons who had a spacious Park Avenue apartment that they opened up each year for a legendary poets' and painters' party. The letter read, "Dear Mr. Violi: I have seen some of your work, and am interested in possibly publishing a book of yours some time. If you are interested, please contact me at the above address. Sincerely yours, Lita Hornick." He contacted Lita and soon after she published *In Baltic Circles*, his first full collection.

Lita liked Paul immensely and ended up asking him to run a reading series at MoMA in the late-'70s and early-'80s. She and Morty also invited Paul and Ann over to their weekend house in Rockland County and to their city apartment for dinner parties, where they met many well-known art world "players." Paul reminisced about Lita's generosity with warmth and affection. After she became infirm—and Morty had died of a heart attack—he kept an eye on her and every so often would escort her to dinner. "I liked them a lot," he explained. "It was the least I could do when she started to decline."

FATHERHOOD AND LIFE UPRIVER

Here—Welcome to Putnam Valley
New York
Population: 9,500
Elevation: Infrequent

—and luster there,
Where pollen so fine it drifted
Through the screen, enaureoled
The cherry wood windowsill.

—from "Envoy" (2005)

In 1972 Paul and Ann were living 60 miles north of the city in Beacon, New York, where Ann headed an English-as-a-second-language program. While in Beacon, their first child, Helen, was born. After a less than enjoyable spell working as a regular substitute teacher, Paul was commuting each day to Manhattan where he found a job working for a fledgling newspaper, *The Herald*. Even though he lived upstate, he continued spending many of his non-working hours downtown socializing and partying with the poets and artists he befriended around Saint Mark's. Since he was on the Metro-North commuter train for hours a day, he used the time to write. Some of *In Baltic Circles* and his next book *Splurge* (1982) were written while commuting. The poem "Boredom" in *In Baltic Circles,* based on a fire he saw through the train window one evening, is about the endless hours shuttling between the Hudson Valley and Manhattan.

After two years working at *The Herald*, Paul landed a good job as the managing editor of *Architectural Forum*. With a master's in special education, Ann found a job teaching at-risk children in West-chester, so they relocated to Briarcliff Manor, where they rented a small cottage on a large picturesque estate. In 1977 they bought a house in Putnam Valley, several miles north of Peekskill. Shortly thereafter their son, Alexander, was born, though with serious con-genital health problems, which caused a stressful few years and near-constant worry. When I asked Paul (via email) to describe the house in which he and Ann raised their two children, he responded in the voice and form of a Pennysaver real estate advertisement. Those familiar with his poetic oeuvre will attest that this is classic Violi, taking an innocent textual form and poetizing it:

> As a real estate ad in the Pennysaver might generously say: 2–3 story cedar shake, 3-bedrooms, spiral stair to guest room below, laundry room, office, living room, tile-floor dining area, 2 skylights, fully equipped kitch, 1 1/2 bath, fireplace, slate-floor screen porch, backyard patio.
>
> Chipmunk condos, i.e. stonewalls, dry or masonry, terrace the ledge the house sits on and cross the sloping "lawn" (mostly weeds and ground cover: myrtle and pachysandra). The house and small piece of property are almost completely shaded by a canopy of (90'+?) oaks from which crows torment the occupants and squirrels scramble. Split logs are usually stacked in sloppy cords next to a small vegetable garden that defies the shade. An 8x8 tool shed, once a children's playhouse, is slowly falling apart at the seams.

In the poem "At The Cottage of Messer Violi" (1998), Paul humorously described his Putnam Valley home in more detail. The first few stanzas read:

> The mailbox, painted dark blue,
> sits atop a tilted cedar post.
> It has a little red flag to one side
> and it is altogether remarkable.
>
> The Toyota in the driveway
> is very old and is said
> to have come from Japan.
>
> There is in the hallway
> An immense dogfood bowl.
> It is made of iridescent pink plastic.
> It is, as I have said, immense
> and it is hideous.
>
> In the kitchenette is a statuette
> of Ceres, Goddess of Wheaties.
>
> The dishwasher is a Kenmore
> and altogether worthy of praise.

I asked if buying a house in Putnam County and having two small mouths to feed hampered his social and aesthetic—poetic—life. Paul explained that having a family was inspiring and fulfilling and that he just went out there and did what he needed to do. He vehemently rejected W.B. Yeats' dichotomy between the life and the work, insisting that the two actively feed one another. "Energy is energy, and experience generates experience, and if you're writing you're writing," he explained. "I wanted it all. It wasn't a dichotomy. I wanted a family; I wanted children; I wanted a job; and I wanted to write. That Yeatsian perfection of a life or perfection of an art—I don't buy it and I don't think he did either. You learn a great deal about life by having a family, profoundly so."

Becoming a father marked a new beginning—and a pleasant one at that. Paul expressed great pride in his two children, who live remarkably different lives. At the time of our interviews, Helen, who had a Ph.D. in botany and lived with her husband in Florida, was doing scientific fieldwork in the Everglades. Alexander, unmarried, was a musician, sound engineer, actor, stage manager, personal trainer, and occasionally a model (having had some success in Japan). He was easily recognizable at Paul's readings, consistently being the only person in the crowd with many tattoos, a dyed Mohawk, and facial piercings. Paul reminisced about how witty his son was when he was little. For example, at the age of three Alex was standing on a dock looking at fish through the water and referred to them as "wobbly boys." "Look at those wobbly boys," he said with a smile. Paul later used the image in a poem.

Helen and Alexander appear in Paul's poetry—usually in anecdotes that convey his abiding love of fatherhood. The poem "Little Testament," written shortly after Paul's fortieth birthday and modeled on a mock testament written by the fifteenth-century French poet François Villon, includes a few of these touching anecdotes:

> *Item*: To my son, Alexander,
> I bequeath with love and admiration
> The Arc de Triomphe.
> And here's why:

To commemorate
the golden attitude you displayed
in the first moments of your life,
the magnificent arc you made
when the doctor
held you aloft in the cold air
and you twisted and turned,
scattering everyone
in the delivery room
as you pissed all over us.

Helen is mentioned shortly after:

Item: To my daughter, Helen,
I leave a prime Elysian lot,
that island-meadow
you rode into
late one afternoon
and let your horse wade at will,
stir up wildflower
and milkweed
in the purpling blue,

so that the silver seed
hovered far around you,
made you smile
amid innumerable smiles
and raised in a casual swarm
years of waves and glinting wings.

POETIC TURNING POINT

We, the naturally hopeful,
Need a simple sign
For the myriad ways we're capsized.
We who love precise language
Need a finer way to convey
Disappointment and perplexity.

—from "Appeal to the Grammarians" (2007)

Paul's second collection of poems, *Splurge*, published in 1982 by Bill Zavatsky at SUN, was seen by Paul as a poetic turning point—or at the very least a more realized version of what he began in *In Baltic Circles*. He wrote the following to me in an email about the book: "I used to think *Splurge* was a big change, but now I'm not so sure. Flipping through *In Baltic Circles* I see poems in various forms and characters: excerpts from imaginary magazines, calendars, diaries, blurbs, mock travelogues, realistic narratives, surreal travelogues and narratives, magazine galleys, reportage, anecdotal pieces, take-offs on famous poems, distorted sonnets, mock tanka and haiku, gratuitous jokes. All seem to be continued—to better effect, I like to think—in *Splurge* and later books. One thing that fortunately fell away was the misty, mushy obscurity."

The first poem in the collection, "One for the Monk of Montaudon," was inspired by translations of troubadour poets. Paul came across a collection of songs about likes and dislikes written by a monk from Montaudon. The collection enthralled him. As he explained it: "I thought I could write a long lyrical poem using that concept of a list, a catalogue really, but make it move like a celebratory ode.... So, I included things I didn't like in addition to things I did like; and what got me going was writing about things I didn't like ... like Mormon Architecture ... as if I did ... and that got me rolling." The poem reflects a deep appreciation for the incidental moments that fill up life, elevating the quotidian to something magical:

> And the sight of a cat, undisturbed,
> curled in the sunlight, pleases me;
> or ketchup smears on table mats
> of Venezuela and its hideous flowers;
> or the sight of boys splattering peaches
> against an ancient stone wall.
>
> I just like to sit back and take it all in,
> watch the sea and sky move together
> like memory and imagination,
> move me out of a dripping indolence
> to a dripping cathedral, like Chartres,
> ("walls of glass, roof of stone")
> where I can stand outside, see
> whatever a summer sky can do, doing it all at once...

Although *Splurge* was met with positive reviews—even getting a spot of national attention with a laudatory review by David Lehman in *Newsday* that characterized Paul as "one of the most inventive poets around"—the '80s found him scrambling around for employment. For starters, *Architectural Forum* folded in 1974. A series of deflating jobs working for various commercial or trade magazines left Paul with a displeasing taste in his mouth. Most notable was the period he spent working for a magazine called *Merchandizing Weekly*. Though the job came with the perk of flying around the country, it required him to write about "fucking washing machines sales."

Paul began looking around for work as a teacher. Earlier, a few of his students at The Poetry Project who were college professors had encouraged him to consider teaching. And so he began using his contacts to find jobs. Like many college adjuncts, he began piecing together as many classes and workshops as he could, beginning with a job teaching at Bloomfield College in New Jersey, followed by workshops for Poets & Writers, Poets-in-the-Schools, and classes at Scarsdale Teacher's Institute, SUNY Purchase, Empire State College, Mercy College, Pace University, Dalton School, Sing-Sing Prison, Stevens Institute, and New York University. The experience of as many as nine classes dispersed across multiple campuses (several in different states) was draining physically. He very much enjoyed the teaching despite the logistical absurdity of it all. Besides, if he felt tired, cigarettes and coffee helped do the trick. Not temperamentally suited for corporate business, Paul felt that writing poetry and teaching pulled things together, giving his life a fullness and integrity where previous occupations fell short. He also liked the ever-changing schedule, which abated his dread of routine.

AFFILIATION WITH KENNETH KOCH

Some people have done you great favors.

—from "Dry Spells" (1981)

Paul met Kenneth Koch through Tony Towle in the early '70s but didn't get to know him well until the early '90s. In 1993 Paul was asked by friends in England to curate an exhibit for a museum in Ipswich. The idea came to him to feature Kenneth's collaborations with painters. He phoned Kenneth and was pleased by his enthusiastic response. The two ended up traveling to Ipswich together and then, after the opening, arranged two weeks of readings around England, which was great fun for both. At one point they were driving north with their British hosts and Kenneth decided that to pass the time they would play a game Kenneth invented (extemporaneously) called "Merit." The game was a parody of Sunday morning talk shows, which meant that when it was your turn to speak you had to be dull and uninteresting. The job of the others was to ask you a question to which you gave a response that would then be evaluated according to whether it had *some* merit; *certain* merit; or it *had* merit (and the duller it was the higher the rating). Paul was sitting in the backseat and was rather hung-over because they'd been drinking late the night before—even managing to get themselves kicked out of a pub. It was Kenneth's turn to ask Paul a question:

> And he had asked me this question about teaching and I gave him this answer and he turns around from the front seat and stares at me for about five seconds and he says, "You're *really* a teacher, aren't you?" And I had just given this answer showing complete jadedness about grading papers and things academic. And then when we got back, I don't remember how long after, but he asked me to teach a class on Eliot because he was going to be out of town.

Paul walked into the class on the appointed day and was astonished to find himself in front of an auditorium of Columbia students. Kenneth's courses were wildly popular; over the years he had assumed legendary status within the English Department. The students sat there ready to hear Paul's take on T.S. Eliot. As he explained it, "I remember teaching this class and I was startled at the end because the students applauded. Soon after, Kenneth sent a case of champagne, and then he phoned and asked me to teach a course called

"Imaginative Writing." It was called "imaginative" by Kenneth to avoid the self-absorption so common in workshops. The course also had a strong literature component. Because Paul also shared ambivalent feelings about excessively self-referential poetry, Kenneth pegged him as the right man to teach the course. And when a vacancy opened in 2000, Kenneth asked if Paul might like to teach the class permanently.

The class, however, was cancelled after Kenneth died in 2002 at the age of 77. The English Department, which took issue with the fact that it was billed as an "imaginative" class, moved it across campus to the Creative Writing Program. Paul was unhappy about this. No longer able to choose the students he wanted, he was forced to take any student who signed up, which often led to a workshop of fifteen or more. But wanting to keep an institutional affiliation with Columbia, he taught for two years under these conditions. Luckily, he was approached by Michael Rosenthal of the English Department, who told him that he was welcome to come back to the English Department to teach literature seminars, provided that he promised not to teach creative writing. Happily, Paul returned to the English Department and began teaching seminars based upon departmental needs, which included courses on Satire, Modern American Poetry, and early twentieth-century British poetry.

REGRETS AND ONGOING STRUGGLES

And when the smoke alarm,
its battery worn down,
began to beep, the signal
at first indistinguishable
from the birdcalls

but then growing louder,
triumphantly monotonous
in their absence, I remained
Three down:
A man of my word.
And that word is
Fifty-five across: Disingenuous.

　　　　　—from "Wet Bread and Roasted Pearls" (1993)

Toward the end of our second interview, I asked Paul about life struggles. Up to that point I had focused on events surrounding the emergence of his artistic identity. Despite being warned by a mutual friend that it would be difficult to wrangle personal information out of Paul, especially for a dissertation that could potentially be published, I had found Paul forthcoming on almost every question I asked. When it came to life struggles, however, he was vague in his responses. It soon became obvious to me that there were things that he simply wasn't going to share. One of my questions was in response to the *Pataphysics* interview he did with the Australian editor Leo Edelstein. In it Paul mentions a period of time during which he was mourning. The prompting question was: "How do you go about finding material for your work? Do you pay attention to your dreams?" Here is Paul's ironic response in full:

> As for dreams—I rarely have memorable ones, or any that make me think there's a nascent poem in one. What I imagine is generally more interesting than what I dream. My dreams are either too explicit, often enjoyably so, or obviously symbolic. For instance, I was mourning recently and I had two dreams that struck me as extensions or

enactments of the loss I was feeling and suppressing. In one I found myself searching through fallen leaves that were inside my house. I was on my hands and knees on a stone tile floor, reaching under leaves, looking for something I'd lost and was unable to grasp. I was bereft but calmly determined. The leaves were crisp, some were lank, freshly fallen, and they were piling up fast. I finally grabbed a broom to clear them away but the more I swept the more there were and there was no telling how they were entering the house and the whole dream plot was a re-enactment of a realization, of the irretrievable. Days later in the second dream I was trying and failing to understand, to decipher a language that I couldn't use to articulate the sorrow I felt. I suspected it might be English, but the words weren't understandable, no arrangement made syntactical sense. Every attempt to make a statement turned into questions. I was questioning the very language and there were no answers; whatever language it was, ultimately all of it was reduced to a pile of ashes, except for these newly forged question marks, very large shiny metal question marks that lay in the ashes. I noticed they had a somewhat elegant design. So, to answer your question: No, I rarely derive poems from dreams.

When I asked whether he cared to specify what it was he was mourning, he responded "No, not today." Consequently, I made a decision to couch my subsequent questions in general terms—asking him to share a story about a period of time that was especially challenging. Paul answered my version of this query in honest, yet general, terms: "You take it as it comes. Either something good comes along and takes you—helps shift your attention, or something worse comes along.... Life is fast...."

Wanting more detail but careful to avoid pushing him too far and compromising the trust I was beginning to earn, I thought it better to skip specifics and ask about his method for dealing with life's tragedies. Paul responded, "You know that phrase 'above all, endure'? There's a little truth to that. Simply to withstand things is a virtue. In other words, the crudest or simplest virtue would be strength. You realize that there's something to be said for just being able to withstand things, because otherwise whatever it is that you need to deal with won't be available if you're reduced to a mess and you're no good to anyone else. Generally, human beings are pretty resilient. I mean everyone gets ambushed ... and others often have worse problems." When asked whether therapy ever played a role in his own process of getting "up off the floor," he said it hadn't—a fact he chalked up to either culture or genetics. "Certain people are made certain ways," he explained. And on a philosophical note: "You mold yourself ... as a result of looking at what you're made of—or how you act—in hopes of either changing the way you are, or staying the way you are. So, introspection is important. But self-absorption is something else ... especially in terms of whining or complaining. I mean I can complain, sure ... but not in public." I asked if this was why he avoided personal confessions in his poetry. Paul took a moment and then answered:

> Poems are based on feelings. And whether those feelings
> are conveyed in a personal sense or as a product of what
> the imagination can turn those feelings into: that's the
> beauty ... that's the pleasure of writing poems. I mean,
> your personal feelings are crucial material, but you want

to make something out of it. Otherwise where's the challenge? I mean, just writing things down the way they are, you're more of a scribe of your self-absorption as opposed to, say, making something that didn't exist before, or by taking something in a different direction. By doing that you become more inclusive; and you can do more with it. Creativity is liberating, an extension of one's self.

Paul did mention that there were some ways that he thinks he could have been a better husband and father, but was careful to point out the futility of coming down too hard on himself. "I look back and wonder if I could have been a better father or a better husband. But of course you want to do some things differently in retrospect. You do the best you can. It's nice to kick yourself in the head once in a while, but not too often."

Paul was acutely aware of the important role that humor has played not only in his poetry but also on his outlook: "I think being a human being, things happen to you. You have a sense of the absurd; you have a sense of your own shortcomings; you have a sense of how things could have gone differently if … if … if…. If you believe in freewill—which I do—you have to have a sense of humor. And I think my humor is based on the contradictory aspects of my own nature as well as the way things happen. Good things happen; great things happen; sad, tragic things happen. I think my humor is tied in with that. And if it's harsh at times it's because I'm pretty harsh on myself; but if it's benign that's because I have an understanding of myself as a mere mortal."

Poetry for Paul operated in a way that's analogous to humor and absurdity. As he wrote in the poem "Dry Spells" (1981), "You have a deep sense of the way / propriety and absurdity complement each other." Both poetry and humor can be a means by which to transform the raw material of living into something celebratory—or, at the very least, into something palatable. They provide a way of converting regret or sadness into something larger, and life affirming.

THE FUTURE

> There it is again, the future,
> and it looks the same as the last time I saw it.
> —from "Melodrama" (1981)

Paul was pragmatic when I asked about his hopes for the future. Although he envisioned writing at least one considerably long poem and hoped to publish a selected poems with a major house, his primary concerns were financial in nature: "I want to clear the deck, and make sure that everything's right for my family. I don't want to leave my family any trouble to take care of. You want to set things right and get things in order." I asked if he ever thought about his own death, and he joked that he increasingly did but only as a result of pharmaceutical ads on TV. Finally, I asked if he believed that there was such a thing as a good death—to which he answered that he wasn't sure that such a thing existed.

I successfully defended my dissertation roughly ten months after my last formal interview with Paul. We passed an earlier version of this bio back and forth and met once for dinner in January or February of 2010. To celebrate my Ph.D., Paul, Charles, and Tony invited me to dinner at Café Loup. They insisted upon paying my bill, and Paul patted me on the back as he left for the hour-plus drive home to Ann in Putnam Valley. Before he took off, several of his New School students spotted him and clustered around our table with beaming grins.

At some point that summer I ran into a mutual friend who had seen Paul for dinner and drinks. The friend told me that Paul looked grayer, thinner, and hadn't touched any of the fries that he'd ordered with his hamburger. We both chalked it up to the fact that his daughter, Helen, had recently given birth to twins and that Paul was taking preventative health measures to ensure that he'd be around long enough to watch them grow up. The following March I received a phone call from another friend who asked if I'd heard from Paul lately. No, I told him, I hadn't, but was meaning to get back in touch. "You should hurry," the friend said. "Paul's dying of pancreatic cancer but wants as few people to know about it as possible. He was diagnosed in early January." I emailed Paul later that day, not mentioning any knowledge of his terminal condition. We had several email exchanges over the month that followed about poetry and my plans to rework the dissertation and publish it. Paul Violi died at Hudson Valley Hospital in Cortland Manor, New York, on April 2, 2011.

WORK

Always up for a beer and a good laugh, Paul Violi was generous, witty, warm, and energetic, and he attracted and charmed people over the years. A cluster of memorials in the months following his death from pancreatic cancer prompted an outpouring of affection from stunned family members, friends, fellow poets, and students. A private man, Paul kept his diagnosis, which he had known about since January of 2011, from all but a small circle of friends and his family. The day after his death on April 2nd, Tony Towle and Charles North sent out an email to his friends, colleagues, and former students informing them. The testimonials that poured in over the weeks and months that followed celebrated the various facets of his expansive personality. He was a family man and an epic socializer, a gregarious worker and reclusive writer, a great humorist and quiet dreamer. Paul travelled the world but had a regional quality to him that fit comfortably in the Hudson Valley, where Ann and he raised their two children. Whether chopping wood in a plaid shirt, or sipping wine in a sports coat at a book launch, Paul possessed a genial ease that women loved and men respected.

Paul knew from an early age that he was a writer, composing his first story at the age of thirteen. After realizing that he had borrowed the plot from Jack London's "To Build a Fire," he moved to verse and mostly stayed there. He liked the intensity of poetry and was initially drawn to the sentimental quatrains of the Irish poet and friend of Byron, Thomas Moore (1779–1852), but found lasting literary heroes in the satirical poets of the eighteenth and early nineteenth centuries and the early modernists. Paul couldn't say why it was he'd always felt he was a writer, but quoted the Roman poet Juvenal's phrase, *cacoethes scribendi*, which translates as "an irresistible urge to write." It was something he'd always felt at home doing. Consequently, it didn't bother him that most of his adult life was spent bouncing from one job to another. As long as he could provide for his family, the absence of an all-consuming career meant that he had more time to read, write, and hang out with his writer friends.

As a reader, Paul was generally unimpressed by a good deal of modern poetry, whether the "deadening" language exercises of LANGUAGE poetry, or the self-aggrandizements of confessional work. On several occasions during our interviews he voiced a particular distaste for poetry that was too serious or self-referential. "You get these poets, and I mean all the time," he explained wryly, "and they're funny, charming, complex people. But for some reason when they get up to read it's always in a serious, self-obsessed voice. And then as soon as they're done the voice disappears, which leaves you wondering what happened to the rest of them!" Paul lamented that current literary directions seemed to undervalue the craft and intelligence it takes to either surprise people or make them laugh; the major journals, magazines, and poetry presses were publishing work that languished in real and manufactured trauma, as if life weren't traumatic enough. He felt similarly about so-called activist poetry. "Don't get me wrong," he said one evening over beers at the KGB Bar in Manhattan's East Village. "I'm all behind nuclear disarmament, but I don't need to read a book-length poem to be convinced."

Enthralled by the ethos of experimentation that pervaded the New York School, Paul mined day-to-day experience for poetic material, following William Faulkner's notion that the writer's job was "to create out of the materials of the human spirit something that did not exist before." Materials existed in everyday happenings like ordering a sandwich at a deli, and within seemingly innocent textual forms like the index of a biography, television listings, or an apology note left on a car after a fender bender. As he put it, "Everyday goings-on, or reading, especially history, provide a lot of nuggets, something that sets me off."

His objective wasn't merely to reflect upon the value of his experiences, but to transpose those experiences into something beyond the realm of personal concern. Otherwise, poetry ran the risk of becoming a testament to one's self-absorption. His frequently anthologized poem "Index" is a good example of his general method of making a poem. The idea came to him while reading the longwinded autobiography of "an egregiously self-indulgent man" whose name he conveniently claimed to have forgotten. Paul couldn't help but notice that the author's egotism had even seeped into the index. "A different character came to mind," he explained, "one who was not quite the master of his fate, and an index, with its fragmentary lines, suggested a way to catch both the quick, haphazard changes such a character would endure and his increasingly scrambled perception of them. As I assembled the poem it began to resemble a chronology." The poem lampoons the twists and turns of an egomaniacal artist's struggle with his own faltering legend and by doing so implicitly pokes fun at the figure of the celebrity artist in contemporary culture.

Paul's imaginative gift was most apparent in this ability to create new poetic forms from familiar linguistic contexts. In a *Newsday* review of *Splurge,* David Lehman pointed out this aptitude: "Paul Violi is the most inventive poet around. His poems can take on the form of television listings ('Triptych') and zany definitions ('Rifacimento'); he can speak with the voice of a veteran fortune-teller ('Dry Spells') or that of a racetrack announcer ('Exacta'). The results are vital, brash, and often very funny" (*Newsday*, 12/19, 1982). Humor and absurdity are defining features of his work, and characterize the jovial way he learned to read his work publically. More than any of his poet friends, perhaps excluding Billy Collins, Paul was a crowd pleaser and his readings could easily reduce a room to sidesplitting laughter. Take the end of "Counterman" from *Overnight* (2008), the last collection of poems he published in his lifetime. The first half of the poem chronicles the speaker's difficulty ordering a simple "roast beef on rye, with tomato and mayo" from the man working the deli counter. The customer behind him has more luck despite a comically outlandish order:

> Roast beef on whole wheat, please,
> With lettuce, mayonnaise and a center slice
> Of beefsteak tomato.
> The lettuce splayed, if you will,
> In a Beaux Arts derivative of classical acanthus,
> And the roast beef, thinly sliced, folded
> In a multi-foil arrangement
> That eschews Bragdonian pretensions
> Or any idea of divine geometric projection
> For that matter, but simply provides
> A setting for the tomato
> To form a medallion with a dab
> Of mayonnaise as a fleuron.
> And—as eclectic as this may sound—
> If the mayonnaise can also be applied
> Along the crust in a Vitruvian scroll
> And as a festoon below the medallion,
> That would be swell.
>
> You mean like in the Cathedral St. Pierre in Geneva?

Yes, but the swag more like the one below the rosette
At the Royal Palace in Amsterdam.

You got it.
Next.

Despite a lifelong affinity for humor and cleverness, Paul didn't like being introduced at readings as "funny" and nothing else. And anyone familiar with his eleven books knows that in addition to being comical, his work is at times tragic, philosophical, and touchingly reflective. Some poems of his are capable of strong passion, and others of surprising tenderness. The coda to his long poem "Sputter and Blaze," for instance, demonstrates the rich emotional ecology that he was capable of achieving:

Now on this cool narrow lake
your absence at evening
below the immeasurable in-between of twilight
I lie in parentheses
amused by how I can trace
in the glistening lines of this canoe
such a dear part of you
and between night and day
sweep up an armful of immediate odes
imagining I can lay them
before you and say
here sift through these in the nibbling dark
there are more too many
for me to follow as they drip
off the dwindling light....

Considering that a coda is the concluding part of a statement, the poem's form is significant. Unpunctuated and without a single stanza break, this poeticized finale possesses an openness and verbosity that verges on the comical. Together, the ironic form and tender, image-rich content convey an experience of deep emotional complexity. As a form of life, it is simultaneously tongue-in-cheek and haunting.

A similar depth can be found in my personal favorite, the long poem "Wet Bread and Roasted Pearls," first published in *The Curious Builder* (1993). The poem begins in a specific place—a Metro-North Hudson line commuter train stalled in the long dark tunnel leading into Grand Central Station. Restless, the poet/speaker gazes down at a crossword puzzle in the newspaper that he is absently holding. He begins to fill in the "maze of blanks" while thinking over a recent episode of marital discord, which culminates in a moment of real or imagined erotic reconciliation:

> in darkness and the curve and line
> of your spine, your neck
> your chin, your ears, your
> legs and breasts and my open hands
> —Hands, rough, callused,
> sliding over your taut silk
> they sound like breath.

The poem captures the amorphous, non-linear way that memories surface and coalesce in response to external triggers—illustrating what Tony Towle meant when he wrote of Paul's ability to "[slip] between internal perception and external observation so easily that they become one." An everyday crossword is magically transformed into a template that weaves together disparate and fragmented feelings, thoughts, perceptions, and recollections into a single fold.

Every passing moment, no matter how mundane, was a candidate for inclusion in a poem. And Paul seemed to know from an early age that the more experiences he was able to pack into his life the better his writing would be. Indeed, his life and poetry were reciprocally linked in a feedback loop. He turned to his experiences for poetic material. And so, the more experiences he had the better, actualizing Frank O'Hara's advice to live as variously as possible. The family time he spent with Ann and their children, the dizzying teaching schedule that he kept up through his mid-sixties, the late night dinners with friends and colleagues, the countless cigarette and coffee breaks, and the other pastimes and relationships he pursued around New York City enabled him to find his next poem forming on the horizon. The alternative for him was a creative wasteland, a routinized life of predictable rhythms, stasis, and psychic death.

Whereas the events of his life provided him with material, the act of writing helped him to manage the ups and downs of life. In 2002 Paul published a collection of prose pieces called *Selected Accidents, Pointless Anecdotes*. In many of the sketches, a sense of absurdity defuses the tension of threatening and/or compromising circumstances. Examples include giving a poetry reading to a small audience of "sub-verbal" and "semi-verbal" adults at a community library that yields "a nod and a nervous laugh, a loud snort and two full smiles"; a road rage altercation with an officious urban cyclist while driving up Hudson Street that concludes with the cyclist inadvertently peddling into an open dumpster; and the predicament of teaching a writing workshop and nearly breaking down into hysterics and ridiculing a student who reads a heart-on-the-sleeve piece about a job he had once as a rent-a-clown. Many of Paul's poems mitigate danger and tension in a similar fashion. For instance, "Extenuating Circumstances"

(2007) chronicles a conversation between the poem's speaker and
a police officer after being pulled over for speeding on the Taconic
Parkway. Although a routine traffic stop is not nearly as dangerous
as other obstacles, the Taconic is a notoriously hazardous road with
a high annual mortality rate, and Paul is driving at night through
wintry conditions with several drinks in his system. Despite these
dangers, the poem is brimming with entertaining humor. The second
half reads:

> Never forget that a parkway
> is a work of art, and the faster
> one goes, the greater the tribute
> to its power of inspiration,
> a lyrical propulsion that approaches
> the spiritual and tempts—demands—
> the more intrepid of us
> to take it from there.
> That sense of the illimitable,
> when we feel we are more the glory
> than the jest or riddle of the world
> —that's what kicked in, albeit
> briefly, as I approached
> the Croton Reservoir Bridge.
> And on a night like this, starlight
> reignited above a snowfall's last
> flurry, cockeyed headlights scanning
> the girders overhead, eggshell
> snowcrust flying off the hood,
> hatching me on the wing
> like a song breaking through prose,

the kind I usually sing
through my nose:

So much to love,
    A bit less to scorn.
    What have I done?
    To what end was I born?

To teach and delight.
    Delight … or offend.
Luck's been no lady,
    Truth a sneaky friend.

Got the heater on full blast,
    Window jammed down,
    Odometer busted,
    Speedometer dead wrong:
Can't tell how fast I'm going,
Don't care how far I've gone.

"The jest or riddle of the world" plays off Alexander Pope's "Glory, jest and riddle of the world" (*Essay on Man*, 1734). Written in heroic couplets, Pope's poem was meant to vindicate the ways of God to man. Likewise, Paul exhorts the patrolman to interpret his speeding as a forgivable peccadillo within a divinely perfected order. So much of Paul's work is redemptive in this manner. The travails and mishaps of living are transposed into ripe occasions for laughter, elegance, and loveliness. He rakes and sifts the muck and silt of the world for diamonds that he holds up with a life-affirming grin, challenging his readers to stop taking themselves so seriously when there's so much beauty out there, and so much to laugh and shrug about.

A poem from *Overnight* (2008) called "Brief Lives" is an outstanding example of redemption Violi-style. The piece is based on the life of a Polish dwarf named Joseph Boruwlaski, who was born in 1739 and lived "to be almost 98, a record for a dwarf." The reader learns that he is buried in Durham Cathedral "Under a slab marked JB. / In St. Mary-the-Less Church / A memorial tablet says he faced changes / In fortune with cheerful resignation." The poem then proceeds to itemize events from his remarkable life story—e.g., being taken in by aristocrats after being orphaned at the age of nine; being taught violin by the musical masters of his day; being given a diamond ring by a young Marie Antoinette; being "continuously fondled by ladies" and marrying one; being named a count by King Stanislaus II; touring the courts of Europe and Asia Minor with his wife; and being deserted by his wife, whom he outlives by decades. Here are the final thirteen lines:

> Long after she dies he still complains about his wife,
> How when he annoyed her she would put him
> On a high shelf and leave the room.
> The actor Stephen Kemble (who
> At 476 pounds played Falstaff
> Without stuffing) becomes a dear friend.
> Both of them die on the same day.
> He travels often in his life, as far as Lapland
> And Nova Zembla, where fascinated natives
> Keep him awake day and night,
> And in their songs thank the sun (which they
> Politely decline to believe is a star)
> For allowing them to see this man.

Although I am not suggesting that Joseph Boruwlaski is Paul Violi, there were similarities between the dwarf's story and Paul's—mainly, the epic, fun-loving tone with which the narrative unfolds. Paul tried his best to face changes of fortune with the same "cheerful resignation" that was attributed to Boruwlaski. In Paul's only 9/11 poem, "September 13, 2001" (also from *Overnight*), he takes a cab uptown to teach a class two days after the September 11th terrorist attacks. There's no mention of 9/11; instead, the poem constitutes a reaffirmation of the city at a moment of profound fearfulness and uncertainty. Here it is in its entirety:

"When you leave New York, you're not going anywhere,"
Del tells a bunch of customers leaving The Grange.
Leaving New York...? What a strange notion.
I'm out the door, too, uptown to teach another class.
Cabbies so annoyingly polite they throw me off my stride.
They're stopping at stop signs for Christ's sake.
On Commerce Street a building, narrow, tower-like—I
Never noticed it before—a great flaming rooftop grove
Of birches soaring in the wind. Phoenix...Phoenicity...
Is there such a word? Felix...Felicity—Anyway,
Something for this city to set its watch by.
Uptown early enough for another coffee, I stop
At the West End, keep a weak joke about Oswald
    Spengler
To myself, and ask Jay to translate what he's chalked up
On the slate board behind the bar. *Veni, Vidi, Velcro:*
"I came, I saw, I stuck around."

Despite the unspeakable calamity of 9/11, Paul, the poet, was busy using his imagination to generate affirmative possibilities in a world that teetered on the brink of terror, anxiety, and retributive anger. The message chalked up on the slate board behind the bar, *Veni, Vidi, Velcro* ("I came, I saw, I stuck around"), is a fitting mantra for a man who stuck around and made it okay to laugh again. But behind the laughter, there's an occasional melancholy beneath the work. It's the melancholy of someone who laughs to avoid collapsing into bitterness, silence, or tears. Although subtle, this muted pathos (present more in the totality of poems than in specific images or themes) tempered Paul's tendency toward slapstick.

As he sat in his Putnam Valley office and composed his poems over the years, he busied himself with an existential project that became increasingly vital as the economic and mortal realities of his life became harder to laugh off. As an adjunct at The New School, NYU, and Columbia, there was always a threat of losing a course, which was problematic because Ann and he depended on the income. His son, Alex, who'd been born with congenital brain damage that kept him from ever learning how to read or write, was having trouble finding enough employment to support himself. And Helen, his daughter, was diagnosed with breast cancer and spent the years leading up to Paul's death in and out of remission. She gave birth to twins before Paul died and then ended up dying roughly a year after her father's funeral, leaving Paul's widow, Ann, devastated.

As noted, Paul chose not to discuss personal struggles much during our meandering conversations. Other than alluding to his ongoing financial concerns, and a suggestion that he could have been a better husband and father, he kept his private life to himself. Similarly, his most heartfelt poems, written in response to beautiful and tragic experiences alike, seldom revealed their sources. And his erotic poems never included the name of the beloved or the circumstances that inspired their composition. I pried at times, but never to any avail. Being sensitive to his comfort level, I chose not to push much. But I walked away from our conversations feeling that a good deal had been left unsaid. At first I wondered whether beneath the humor and inventiveness there stretched an uncharted country of struggle and grief that he purposefully kept from his poems. Even if this was the case, however, the poems he chose to write remain a more accurate testament to the shape of his existence than anything lurking in a shadowy realm below.

ABOUT ANDREW McCARRON

A poet, teacher, and hagiographer, Andrew McCarron was born and raised in the Hudson River Valley. He holds a Ph.D. in Social/Personality Psychology and currently chairs the Religion, Philosophy & Ethics Department at Trinity School in Manhattan. His first collection of poetry, *Mysterium,* was published by Edgewise Press in 2011, and his book-length study of Bob Dylan's religious identities is forthcoming from Oxford University Press.

CPSIA information can be obtained at www.ICGtesting.com
Printed in the USA
BVOW02s1845230715

409785BV00011B/5/P